O9-AIG-089

The
WORST-CASE SCENARIO
Survival Handbook:
COLLEGE

The
WORST-CASE SCENARIO
Survival Handbook:
COLLEGE

By Joshua Piven, David Borgenicht, and Jennifer Worick
Illustrations by Brenda Brown

CHRONICLE BOOKS

SAN FRANCISCO

Worst-Case Scenario™ and The Worst-Case Scenario Survival Handbook™ are trademarks of Quirk Productions, Inc.

Library of Congress Cataloging-in-Publication Data available.

ISBN-10: 0-8118-4230-4

ISBN-13: 978-0-8118-4230-3

Printed in China

Typeset in Adobe Caslon, Bundesbahn Pi, and Zapf Dingbats

Designed by Frances J. Soo Ping Chow
Illustrations by Brenda Brown

A **QUIRK** Book
www.quirkpackaging.com
Visit www.worstcasescenarios.com

10 9

Chronicle Books LLC
680 Second Street
San Francisco, California 94107
www.chroniclebooks.com

WARNING

When a life is imperiled or a dire situation is at hand, safe alternatives may not exist. To deal with the worst-case scenarios presented in this book, we highly recommend—insist, actually—that the best course of action is to consult a professionally trained expert, most likely not an academician. But because highly trained professionals may not always be available when the safety or sanity of individuals is at risk, we have asked experts on various subjects to describe the techniques they might employ in these emergency situations. THE PUBLISHER, AUTHORS, AND EXPERTS DISCLAIM ANY LIABILITY from any injury that may result from the use, proper or improper, of the information contained in this book. We do not guarantee that the information contained herein is complete, safe, or accurate, nor should it be considered a substitute for your good judgment, your common sense, or everything your parents ever taught you. And finally, nothing in this book should be construed or interpreted to infringe on the rights of other persons or to violate criminal statutes; we urge you to obey all laws and respect all rights, including property rights, of others, even members of other fraternities and sororities, the faculty and administration, and visiting teams and their mascots.

—The Authors

CONTENTS

I have never let my schooling
interfere with my education.

—Mark Twain

INTRODUCTION

Dozens of images come to mind when you think about college life. Professors. Fraternities. Tweed jackets with suede elbow patches. Parties. Football games. Backpacks loaded with books. Parties. Intense seminars. Sororities. Huge, hushed classrooms filled with students taking tests. Parties. All-night cram sessions. Wool sweaters/surfboards (depending on region). Beverages. A blinking cursor on a blank computer screen. The homecoming parade.

To be sure, heading off to college for the first time is one of life's great milestones. You're finally leaving the nest, heading out on your own to choose your own path. You're ready to learn what it takes to succeed, to explore your inner self, and to figure out what you really want to be. The world is your oyster— if only you can figure out how to shuck it.

Thankfully, first-time college students have a variety of resources at their disposal to help them prepare. Guidance counselors, alumni, faculty advisors, resident advisors, and campus tour guides do their best to give students a sense of what's in store. And when it comes to the basics, they do just fine. They are perfectly capable of preparing you for the more common challenges you'll face at school—how to pick a major, how to add or drop classes, how to improve your study habits, and how to find your way around campus. Your mom can teach you how to do your laundry and heat up canned soup, and your high school teachers should be able to give you the basic study skills you'll need.

But what about when college life takes a sudden turn for the worse?

Who do you go to when you discover you have a nightmare roommate, or when you're served a tray of completely unrecognizable and probably dangerous institutional food? How do you deal with a thoroughly gross dorm bathroom, or open a bottle without an opener? What's the best way to ask your parents for money, and how do you survive the walk of shame? What do you do if you've never attended a class and now you have a test?

That's where we come in.

With expert advice from experienced bartenders, truckers, lifeguards, safety instructors, bail bondsmen, poison control workers, and, of course, professors, admissions officers, and psychologists, among many other experts, *The Worst-Case Scenario Survival Handbook: College* is your guide. It is required reading for every student.

We've organized the book into four sections—Getting Settled, Room and Board, Extracurricular Survival Skills, and Class Survival—and have included an appendix with extra special aids: Because we know that *sounding* smart can be even more important than *being* smart, we've provided an easy-to-use pronunciation guide to philosophers, artists, and writers with weird names. The appendix also includes a useful letter/speech to tell your parents that you've been expelled. And should all else fail, there's a more-or-less realistic-looking diploma (you fill in your name) that you can enlarge on a photocopy machine, frame, and hang.

Whether you're attending a small college or a large university, living in a dorm or off-campus, or are a freshman or a senior, you still must survive your college experience. This book tells you how.

—The Authors

CHAPTER 1
GETTING SETTLED

HOW TO AVOID GOING TO THE WRONG COLLEGE

1 Visit the college during the school year on a day with a regular class schedule.

Visiting during holidays, homecoming, or other times when students are away or not in their normal routine will not give you an accurate picture of everyday life at the school.

2 Observe the students.

- Are the students walking energetically to class while talking animatedly, or are the few students in sight wandering aimlessly?
- Are the students bright-eyed, with glowing complexions, or are they red-eyed, with a pasty pallor?
- Are the students carrying armfuls of books and notebooks, or are they carrying surfboards and coolers?
- Are the students eagerly seeking out professors after class and in the cafeteria, or are the students ducking into doorways and under tables to avoid professors?
- Are students in class paying attention and taking notes, or are they wearing headphones, reading the newspaper, or dozing?

Compare the number of books in the library to the number of seats in the stadium.

3 Evaluate the facilities and surroundings.

- Compare the number of books in the library to the number of seats in the stadium.
- Compare the number of flyers promoting free lectures to the number of flyers promoting spring break getaways.
- Compare the number of nearby art galleries to the number of nearby hair salons.
- Compare the number of nearby bookstores to the number of nearby bars.
- Compare the number of students wearing T-shirts with the school logo to the number of students not wearing any shirt.
- Compare the number of ads in the school newspaper offering "Students Available to Tutor" to the number of ads offering "Research Papers Written—Any Topic."
- Compare the number of times you hear chamber music to the number of times you hear sirens from emergency vehicles.

4 Select your school accordingly.

How to Identify a Party School

⭐ Assess the school's location.

Party schools are often those farthest from urban centers: Such a location necessitates that all social activities occur on campus or in campus-adjacent locations, and therefore there are parties daily due to the lack of other entertainment opportunities. Cities with a warm climate and good beaches are also home to party schools, as many students opt for surfing, sunbathing, and pitchers of margaritas over class.

⭐ Count the number of bars, liquor stores, fraternities, and sororities on or near campus.
The more plentiful the watering holes and Greek organizations, the more likely the students are to party.

⭐ Look for schools with successful sports teams.
Schools with particularly winning sports programs are likely to offer many months of pre- and post-game victory parties. Avoid schools with losing records or sparsely attended games, and those with teams that usually lose the homecoming alumni game.

A warm climate often encourages a party atmosphere.

⭐ **Interview the school's administrators and alumni.**
Talk to the school's local boosters (ask the admissions office for names) about their memories of social activities at the school. If more than three of them recount stories of drinking at 6 A.M. or have no memory of college at all, the school is most likely a party school.

⭐ **Visit the school on a Thursday.**
A good party school will have multiple parties raging on this night. Walk the campus and listen carefully for whoops, yells, and loud music. Look for students staggering, talking loudly, or vomiting in the bushes, all of which are signs of raucous social activity. Enter a fraternity or sorority party. Gatherings without alcohol and centered around a knitting circle or a discussion of nineteenth-century English poetry indicate a college that does not measure up.

Interview the school's administrators.

HOW TO TAKE ON A NEW IDENTITY

College matriculation is the start of a new academic career and, if you so choose, the beginning of your new persona.

Jock

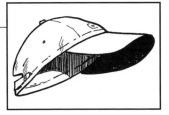

Attire

Wear:
- Baseball cap with school logo
- Sweatpants
- Shorts (if temperature above 50°F)
- Fleece (if temperature under 50°F)
- T-shirt with arms cut off
- Elastic ankle or wrist brace
- Expensive new running shoes or expensive, worn cross-training shoes

Do Not Wear:
- Tweed or plaid
- Nail polish
- Lace or bows
- Leather pants
- Stilettos

Paraphernalia to Carry
- Gym membership card
- Topical pain reliever

- Weight-lifting gloves or belt
- Sports drink, energy bars
- Keys on shoelace around neck
- Large duffel bag with team name

Where to Hang Out
- Field house
- Greek parties
- Gym
- Jock dorm
- Sports bar

Where to Sit in Class
In the back, if you show up

Buzzwords to Use
- Lats
- Quads
- Carbo-loading
- Strength training
- Stats
- Reps
- Scouts

Critical Knowledge
- Mold the brim of your baseball cap into a half circle before wearing it. Wash new hats with bleach and rub a few spots with sandpaper for added authenticity.
- Sprinkle creatine powder on your cereal at breakfast.

Hippie

Attire

Wear:

- Homemade clothes
- Bell bottoms
- Sandals
- Wool socks
- Hemp jewelry
- Tie-dyed T-shirts
- Flowers in hair

Do Not Wear:

- Necktie
- Spandex
- Three-piece suit
- Shoes

Paraphernalia to Carry

- Bootleg cassettes
- Rolling papers
- Frisbee
- Hackey-sack
- Dog

Where to Hang Out

- Park or nature preserve
- Food co-op
- Jam band concert
- Vegetarian café
- Protest

Where to Sit in Class
Indian-style on the desk or floor

Buzzwords to Use
- 420
- Resin, carb
- Set list
- Spun-out
- Bummer

Critical Knowledge
- How to roll your own cigarettes.
- The location of nearest campground to every major stadium and concert venue in North America.
- Jerry Garcia's birthday.

Intellectual

Attire
Wear:
- Glasses
- Rumpled tweed jacket with elbow patches
- Khaki pants or wrinkled long skirt
- Mussed hair
- Bow tie
- Sweater vest

Do Not Wear:
- Sunglasses
- Low-rider jeans

- Thong underwear
- Hair products
- Sweat bands

PARAPHERNALIA TO CARRY
- Pipe
- Umbrella
- Cane or walking stick
- Hefty tome
- Battered leather briefcase

WHERE TO HANG OUT
- Library
- Dorm lounge
- On-campus snack bar
- Professors' offices

WHERE TO SIT IN CLASS
In front row

BUZZWORDS TO USE
- Dissertation
- Orals
- Academic armamentarium
- MCATs, LSATs, GREs
- Phi Beta Kappa, magna cum laude, summa cum laude

CRITICAL KNOWLEDGE
- See "How to Sound Intelligent," page 162.

Foreign Student

ATTIRE
Wear:
- Shirt with obscure logo
- Foreign flag patch on your backpack
- Cologne or perfume
- High-style shoes not sold in this country
- Leather clutch purse (men), large leather shoulder bag (women)

Do Not Wear:
- White socks
- Baseball cap
- American flag pin
- Deodorant

PARAPHERNALIA TO CARRY
- Translation dictionary
- Map of foreign country
- Electrical adapter
- Adult contemporary CDs
- Airmail envelopes

WHERE TO HANG OUT
- The international dorm
- Library
- With other foreign students
- At foreign films

WHERE TO SIT IN CLASS
In the middle, trying (unsuccessfully) to blend in

BUZZWORDS TO USE
- Student visa
- "In your country . . ."
- "How do you say . . . ?"

CRITICAL KNOWLEDGE
- Names of the leaders, major landmarks, and holidays in the country you're pretending to be from.
- Key curse words and phrases in "your language."

HOW TO AVOID A DISASTER MATTRESS

★ Arrive at school early.
Get to your dorm and your room when nobody else is around.

★ Test the mattress.
- **SMELL TEST:** Is this an odor you can live with?
- **COIN TEST:** Bounce a quarter on the mattress. If it has any bounce at all, you have found an exceptional mattress.
- **JUMP TEST:** Leap from floor to bed repeatedly on different areas of the mattress. Will it support your weight, or has the mattress collapsed?
- **SUPINE TEST:** Lie down on the mattress. Does it have a smooth surface, or is it lumpy or sunken?
- **DOUBLE SUPINE TEST:** Lie down with a friend and ask him to roll over, bounce, and sit up. How does your half of the bed respond?
- **FLIP TEST:** Repeat all tests on the other side of the mattress.

★ Find a better mattress.
If the mattresses in your room don't pass the test, check mattresses in other, empty dorm rooms and the dorm storage area. Take the best one, replacing it with yours.

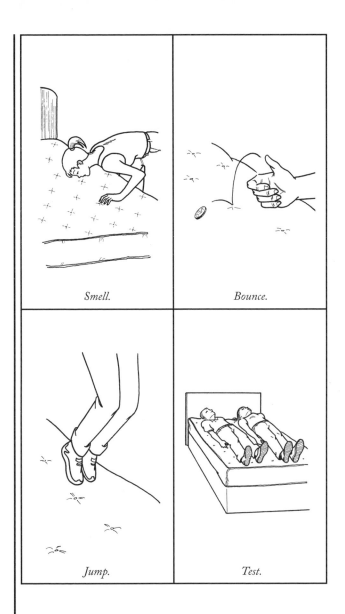

Smell.

Bounce.

Jump.

Test.

how to avoid a disaster mattress

Stake your claim.

Make up the bed you have selected before your roommate arrives. Stack books, clothes, and other personal
items on the bed to further mark your territory.

Be Aware

- Every few months, flip your mattress over or move
  it around so that the head becomes the foot of the
  bed. This will prevent any permanent indentations
  or lumps from forming in the mattress.
- Check with the custodial staff before installing
  your own water bed.

HOW TO DECORATE YOUR ROOM WHEN YOU'RE BROKE

MILK CRATE CHAIR

You will need a square, stackable milk crate; a cloth placemat or your favorite fabric in a similar size; an old magazine; 6 large car-wash sponges; heavy upholstery thread; an upholstery sewing needle; and scissors.

1 Turn the crate upside down.

2 Create the base of the cushion.
Place the magazine on top of the bottom of the crate. Use the scissors to trim the magazine pages so that the magazine rests about ¾ inch from the inside edge of the crate.

3 Arrange 4 sponges on top of the magazine.
Lay the sponges next to one another to form the cushion. You may have to use the scissors to trim them to fit squarely to the top of the crate.

4 Lay the remaining sponges on top of the existing row.
Create a second layer of cushion by centering 2 sponges on top of the first layer.

5 Anchor the placemat to the crate.
Position the placemat on top of the sponges. Using the needle and thread, secure both shorter sides of the placemat to the crate by hooking a single loop stitch through the edge and around a crate grid square.

6 Push down on the placemat.
Compress the sponges until the longer sides of the fabric reach the edges of the crate.

7 Sew the placemat to the crate.
Secure the placemat with a continuous loop stitch around the perimeter of the crate.

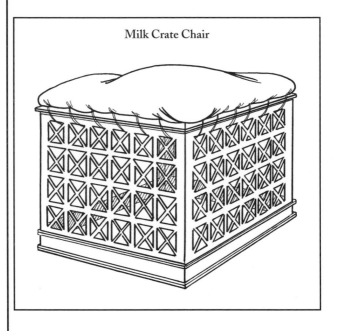

Milk Crate Chair

8 Sit.

You can also use the crate as an ottoman or low stool, or stack it on top of another crate for a desk-height chair.

Be Aware

If you're using your own fabric rather than a place-mat, lay a strip of masking tape $1/4$ inch from the edges around the perimeter of the fabric to prevent fraying before securing the fabric to the crate.

T-Shirt Curtains

To accommodate a window of approximately 4 feet x 4 feet, you will need 13 of your favorite old T-shirts; 1 spool of thread in any color; 1 to 2 spools of iron-on hem tape; 1 spool of picture-hanging wire; 2 medium-weight eyehole screws; 1 manila folder (or similarly stiff paper); a medium-tipped marking pen; a sharp pair of scissors; and a sewing machine.

1 Make a stencil.

Cut the manila folder into a rectangle (9 inches x 12 inches) or a square (10 inches x 10 inches) to make a stencil.

2 Cut the T-shirts into pieces.

Lay a T-shirt on a flat surface for cutting. Put the stencil on the center of the shirt body. Trace the outline of the stencil with the marker on the T-shirt. Lift the stencil off the shirt. With the scissors, cut through

T-Shirt Curtains

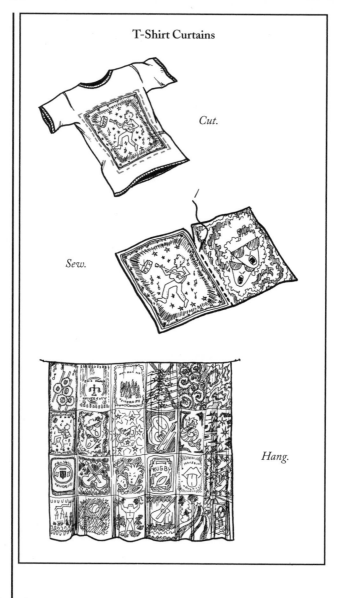

Cut.

Sew.

Hang.

both layers of the T-shirt, following the drawn cut-line. Perform this step on all the shirts.

3 Arrange the pieces to make a curtain.
On the floor or your bed, arrange the pieces next to one another in a pattern you like. Use as many pieces as you need to create a covering a little bit longer and wider than your window.

4 Disassemble the curtain.
Collect your horizontal rows into piles and set them down next to your sewing machine.

5 Sew the pieces together.
Place the front faces of two pieces together and sew, using a medium straight stitch $1/4$ inch from the edge of the mated pieces.

6 Connect the rows.
Sew front face to front face. Make sure any design on the T-shirt pieces is right-side up.

7 Finish the edges.
Once you have sewn the window covering to the desired size, cut the hem tape to size for the perimeter of the covering. Iron on the hem tape along the sides so the tape wraps around the edge, covering the front and back of the edge.

8 Prepare the curtain for hanging.

Facing the front of your window piece, fold back 2 inches of the top edge to form the place to string the picture-hanging wire through. Secure the folded portion by sewing $1/4$ inch along the edge. Cut the wire 1 foot longer than the width of your window opening. Thread the wire through the pipeline you created.

9 Hang the curtain.

With your hand, screw in the eyehole screws at either edge of your window. Hang the window covering by wrapping 6 inches of excess wire through the eyehole hooks.

Be Aware

If you do not have a sewing machine, hem tape, or a needle and thread, use a stapler or duct tape to secure the T-shirt pieces together.

ALTERNATE METHOD:

If you would rather keep your T-shirts intact, run a curtain rod straight through the armholes of as many T-shirts as it takes to cover the width of the window. Repeat this procedure, adding more rows until the window is covered. Smelly, worn T-shirts can be put on the rods to be aired out, thus saving you from having to wash them.

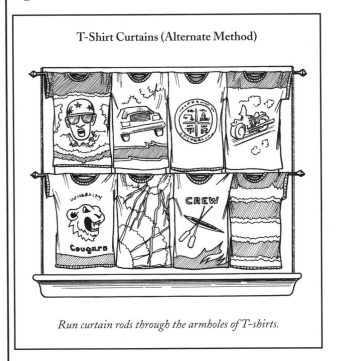

T-Shirt Curtains (Alternate Method)

Run curtain rods through the armholes of T-shirts.

Picture Frame

You will need an empty, transparent jewel case from a CD; a photo; and scissors.

1 Detach the cover of the jewel case at its hinge.

2 Reattach the cover, wrong-side out.
This will form a wide V shape that can stand up on a flat surface.

3 Insert your photo on top of the outer half of the case.
Use the scissors to trim the photo to fit. Add colored paper behind the photo for a more sophisticated look.

4 Display.

CHAPTER 2

ROOM AND BOARD

HOW TO SURVIVE IN A SMALL ROOM

⭐ **Hang mirrors.**
Affix a large mirror to one wall, flush with a corner. Mirrors create the illusion of space: The bigger the mirror, the longer the appearance of the wall and the better the illusion. Place another mirror opposite a window to reflect light.

⭐ **Repaint the room.**
Go light, not white. Light colors give the appearance of spaciousness, but most dorm rooms are painted bright white, which is very antiseptic. Paint the walls a warm shade of off-white (cream or vanilla). If you are prohibited from painting in your dorm, tack up cream-colored sheets to cover drab walls.

⭐ **Use torchiers rather than overhead fluorescent lighting.**
Torchiers, or standing floor lamps, project light toward the ceiling. The light diffuses and bounces back into the room, giving the feeling of spaciousness. Halogen torchiers are economical but can also increase the risk of fire due to the intense heat of the bulb.

⭐ **Furnish sparsely.**
The fewer the belongings, the larger the room appears to be. Decorate with furniture that serves dual purposes, such as a coffee table/storage unit.

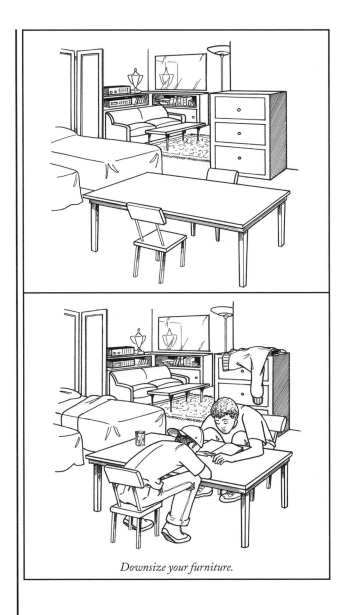

Downsize your furniture.

⭐ **Add small rugs and lamps.**
Use desk lamps and small area rugs to fashion several distinct pools of light and space. When the eye sees multiple separate spaces, the brain is fooled into thinking a room is bigger than it is.

⭐ **Divide the room.**
Use a folding screen or fabric to divide a room or create privacy. Use double-sided tape or thumbtacks to attach a flowing, semi-opaque fabric to the ceiling to partition a room while still allowing light to filter through.

⭐ **Elevate your bed.**
Add valuable storage space by raising your bed off the floor. Use cinder blocks to gain 6 inches of storage room, or build a loft and put your mattress on top of it. Place your desk under the loft to create a cozy workspace.

⭐ **Downsize your furniture.**
Buy children's or other small furniture. This will make the room appear larger. However, you might not be able to sit down.

⭐ **Kick out your roommate.**

HOW TO DEAL WITH A NIGHTMARE ROOMMATE

⭐ Cover foul odors.
Burn incense or spray air freshener to mask your roommate's scent. To better circulate the incense, place it in front of an open window or oscillating fan.

⭐ Secure your possessions in locked storage containers.
To discourage theft or misuse of your belongings, lock as much as possible in safes, military-issue foot lockers, trunks, and other lockable storage containers. Long, flat containers can be placed under your bed for further protection.

⭐ Divide the room in half.
Draw a line down the center of the room to designate your own private space. Remember that you'll have to share the door.

⭐ Wear noise reduction headphones.
Don the headphones anytime your roommate is in the room with you.

⭐ Leave a bar of soap on his pillow.

⭐ Put neglected dirty dishes in your roommate's bed.

★ **Gather long-unwashed clothes into a pile.**
If the pile of dirty clothes isn't remedied after a week, transfer the pile to trash bags and seal tightly to eliminate odors. If the bags remain after several weeks, put them in the trash.

★ **Misalign the satellite dish.**
Disrupt the constant blare of sporting events by redirecting your roommate's satellite dish.

★ **Buy your roommate concert tickets.**
If your roommate never leaves the room, buy him a ticket to an all-day concert, a movie, or a sporting event. Do not ask your roommate if he wants to go; just purchase the ticket—the farther away the event, the better.

Be Aware

If you notice any of the following in your room, you may have a nightmare roommate:

- Giant speakers
- Lack of toiletries
- Machete
- More than 15 stuffed animals

HOW TO DEAL WITH A PROMISCUOUS ROOMMATE

★ Prearrange a "keep out" signal.
Agree that a towel wrapped around the door handle, a hotel-style "Do Not Disturb" sign, or an index card in the doorjamb indicates the room is occupied and being used, and you should stay out for an agreed-upon period of time. Forty-five minutes should be the maximum.

★ Dismantle bunk beds and move your bed far away from his.
You will be less likely to be awakened if your bed frame is not attached to his.

★ Pretend that nothing is happening.
Start a conversation with your roommate as though nothing is going on. Ask questions about how his day has been, what he's planning on doing tomorrow, or what he had for dinner. Talk to his hook-up. "I don't believe that we've ever met before. What is your name? What's your major?"

★ Play your stereo.
Blast loud, raucous music from your stereo to break your roommate's concentration. Avoid sultry songs that will only provide encouragement.

⭐ Watch television.
Wear headphones plugged into your television to block out noise and distract yourself.

⭐ Foil future hook-ups.
Be your roommate's shadow at parties. When it appears that a hook-up may be in the offing, quickly intercede when your roommate is distracted. Mention how great it is that the two have gotten together "in light of his recent condition," then be evasive. Comments such as "I hope you have a better time than the others" and "I expect I'll be seeing more of you since I rarely leave the room" will also discourage the hook-up. If all else fails, tell your roommate that you forgot your keys and ask him to walk you home. If he won't leave with you, ask for his keys. When he returns home, you can choose whether or not to unlock the door.

⭐ Obtain a date of your own.

How to Silence Squeaky Bedsprings

⭐ Lubricate.
When your roommate's bed is not in use, oil the bedsprings and any joints of the bed frame that are visible.

⭐ Tighten the nuts and bolts.
Use a wrench to strengthen the bed's framework.

⭐ Wrap the bed's joints.
Wrap cotton strips or thick socks around the bed's joints to muffle a squeaking sound. Use duct tape to secure the wrapping in place.

⭐ Remove the mattress from the frame.
Encourage your roommate to sleep with the mattress directly on the floor or set it on a thick piece of plywood resting on cinder blocks.

⭐ Wear earplugs.
The bed might still squeak, but you won't notice.

⭐ Make your own bed squeak.

HOW TO DEAL WITH AN UNEXPECTED VISIT FROM YOUR PARENTS

1 Stall for time.

Enlist the help of your roommate or another nearby friend. Ask her to greet your parents and to delay them outside, telling them that you just stepped out of the shower and you need a moment to dry off and dress. This should buy you at least five minutes to get the room ready.

2 Hide all inappropriate items.

Search for objects or people that may cause your parents distress or cause them to reconsider their financial contribution to your college tuition. Hiding these items is your first priority; cleaning can come later, if you have time. Locate and conceal the following:

- beer cans, empty or full
- liquor bottles
- cigarettes (including butts, cellophane wrapping, cigars, ashtrays, lighters, and matches)
- certain magazines, videos, posters, and calendars
- stolen street signs
- firecrackers
- partially clothed members of the opposite sex
- women's undergarments (if male)
- men's undergarments (if female)

- completed exams that belong to anyone but you
- newly acquired expensive electronic equipment
- travel brochures
- parking tickets
- all forms of birth control

3 Air out the room.
Open the window, no matter what the outside temperature. Douse a sock with cologne, perfume, a styling product, or another heavily scented liquid that will mask the odor of any smoke, mold, or musty laundry in the room. Swing the sock in a circular motion above your head while walking around the room.

4 Check the time.
Your parents will grow suspicious if you keep them waiting for too long. Determine whether you have time to continue to clean up your room.

5 Stow your clothes.
Gather all of your dirty clothes into the middle of the floor. Shove as many articles as possible into your hamper or laundry bag. Stand on top of the hamper to force the clothes down so that you can add more on top. When you run out of room, put the rest of your clothes under the bed, stack them on the floor of the closet, or use them as makeshift furniture: Sit on the pile to create an indentation. Cover the pile with a sheet, tucking the sides of the sheet under the pile. The laundry now looks like a beanbag chair.

Gather clothes
into a pile.

Create an
indentation.

Cover the pile.

6 Make your bed.
Remove the comforter from the bed. Throw flat items like magazines, books, and papers onto your mattress, taking care not to pile them. Fluff the comforter to increase thickness, then tuck it under the mattress to secure. Arrange pillows on top.

7 Check the time.
If you've kept your parents waiting for more than five minutes, skip to step 9. Blame any remaining mess on your roommate. If you have time, continue to step 8.

8 Sweep away clutter.
Shoes, toiletries, food, mail, dirty plates, pizza boxes, hangers, dead plants, empty soda cans or bottles, and any other unsightly clutter can be jammed under your bed or into the closet on the floor or a high shelf. Carefully close the door. Do not open the closet while your parents are in the room.

9 Primp.
Put on deodorant or apply an odor-concealing perfume or aftershave. Put on clean clothes or, if unavailable, turn dirty attire inside out. Wet and comb your hair to give yourself a just-showered look.

10 Greet your parents.
Enthusiastically embrace your parents. Tell them that it is a wonderful surprise to see them. Make it clear that you have a lot of studying to do before the day is over so that you can keep the visit short. Allow your

parents to make a quick survey of your room, then suggest going out for a tour of campus and some coffee. Gently but forcefully lead them away as quickly as possible.

Be Aware
Use caution when opening the closet door after a rush-cleaning job. Tuck your chin to your chest, curl one arm over your head for protection, and expect an avalanche.

HOW TO HIDE THINGS IN YOUR DORM ROOM

SMALL ITEM

⭐ Use an old textbook.
Stash cash between pages. For other items, make a secret compartment.
- Open the book to page 50 or beyond.
- Use a razor blade or a sharp knife to cut a square hole in the center of the book. Use a metal ruler to guide you, and keep repeating your cut lines to go deeper and deeper.
- Remove the square cut-out pages.
- Put the item in the compartment.
- Reshelve the book.

⭐ Use a potted plant.
- Seal the item in a plastic bag.
- Dig a hole several inches deep in the soil.
- Bury the bag.

⭐ Construct a beer can safe.
- Using a nail or pen, poke a small hole in one side of a beer can, near the bottom. Drink or discard the contents.
- Use scissors or tin snips to cut away the side of the can with the hole, leaving the top and bottom intact.

Select a thick book.

Cut vertically.

Cut horizontally.

Remove pages.

- Stash valuables in the can and place it on a wall covered with other, similar cans. Make sure the hole in the can faces the wall.

⭐ Use electrical outlets.

This location is suitable for very small and dry items only.

- Use a screwdriver to unscrew the switch plate that surrounds a light switch or electrical outlet.
- Insert the item in the wall cavity.
- Replace the plate.

⭐ Use shampoo bottles.

- Seal the item in a waterproof bag.
- Hide the bag in a bottle of shampoo.
- Keep your bathroom items separate from your roommate's to avoid detection.

⭐ Use baseboards.

- Pry a small section of baseboard away from the wall, using a hammer and chisel or flat screwdriver.
- Use the hammer to pound a hole in the drywall just above the floor, in an area that will be concealed by the baseboard.
- Stash the item in the hole.
- Replace the baseboard by wedging it in place.

LARGE ITEM

★ Camouflage.

Pile dirty or damp clothing on the item to be hidden. Make sure the pile looks and smells sufficiently unappealing to prevent scrutiny.

★ Use a feather pillow.

Depending on the size and weight of the item, you may be able to stash it in a feather pillow. Unzip the pillow and bury the item in the middle. Make sure all hard edges are well covered with several inches of feathers. Re-zip and cover with a dirty pillowcase to deter inspection.

★ Use your roommate.

If you suspect you will be the subject of a search (particularly a search by a thieving roommate), hide valuables among your roommate's possessions. Make sure the hidden item is well concealed in the back of a closet, under her bed, or in another location she is unlikely to visit regularly. Check periodically to be certain the hidden item has not been detected.

HOW TO SURVIVE THE DORM BATHROOM

Toilet

★ Clean the seat.

Wipe the toilet seat with baby wipes, or spray the seat with disinfectant.

★ Use a seat cover.

Bring a child-size life preserver to place on the toilet seat (be sure the straps hang outside of the bowl). Alternatively, completely cover the seat with paper seat covers or at least four layers of toilet paper.

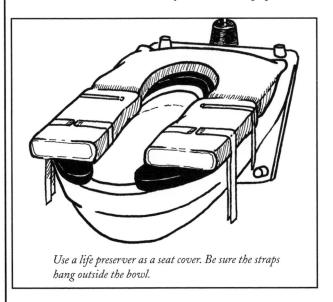

Use a life preserver as a seat cover. Be sure the straps hang outside the bowl.

Squat.
Tie your belt or necktie around the cubicle latch, hold on to the other end, and squat over the toilet seat, never touching the surface.

 Find alternative facilities.
Scope out other bathrooms on campus for cleanliness and privacy. The admissions office generally has a nice public restroom for prospective students and their parents. The library is probably clean and quiet immediately after opening. Avoid athletic facilities.

Be Aware
If toilet paper is nowhere to be found, use napkins, paper towels, coffee filters, day-old newspapers (the ink will be dry), pages from a telephone book, old blue books, foreign currency (after checking the exchange rate), literary magazines on uncoated paper, glossy magazines, or pages from a textbook.

SHOWER

 Shower at off hours.
Shower in the middle of the night or at midday to avoid a wait and ensure hot water. Shower at the gym during—not after—a team practice or at off hours.

 Protect your feet.
Never touch the floor with your bare feet. Wear flip-flops, clogs, or other elevated or enclosed footwear. Shoes with rubber soles will prevent slipping.

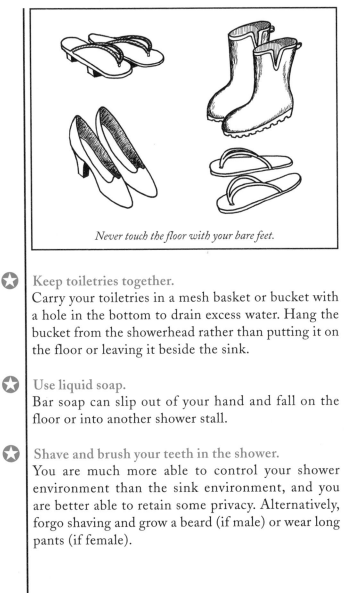

Never touch the floor with your bare feet.

⭐ Keep toiletries together.
Carry your toiletries in a mesh basket or bucket with a hole in the bottom to drain excess water. Hang the bucket from the showerhead rather than putting it on the floor or leaving it beside the sink.

⭐ Use liquid soap.
Bar soap can slip out of your hand and fall on the floor or into another shower stall.

⭐ Shave and brush your teeth in the shower.
You are much more able to control your shower environment than the sink environment, and you are better able to retain some privacy. Alternatively, forgo shaving and grow a beard (if male) or wear long pants (if female).

★ Date someone who lives off campus. Shower there whenever possible.

Be Aware

- Dormitory showers are prime areas for pilfering. Leave valuables in your room. Put your keys on a key chain that you can wear around your wrist while showering. Lock your cell phone, pager, jewelry, money, laptop computer, and all other expensive items in your room.
- Dorm bathrooms are often crowded and unpleasant. To avoid the bathroom, use your room to:
  - Shave, preferably with an electric razor
  - Clean your hair with a dry shampoo
  - Brush your teeth with a bottle of water
  - Clean your face with cold cream and a tissue
  - Apply makeup
  - Add hair product and blow-dry hair
  - Mask body odor with talcum powder, underarm deodorant, or deodorant body spray

HOW TO AVOID DOING LAUNDRY

⭐ Air out your dirty clothes.
Hang dirty clothes in your room. Spritz key areas with a spray deodorizer. Turn on an oscillating fan or use a blow-dryer to dry and refresh the garments.

⭐ Wear dark colors.
Dark-colored clothing will usually hide stains better than lights or whites. However, wearing dark colors in hot weather may increase perspiration and its resultant odors. Camouflage and heavily patterned clothing is also effective in hiding stains.

⭐ Borrow clothes.
Befriend people your size and ask for loans.

⭐ Wear clothes inside out.
When clothing becomes stained, turn it inside out and put it back on; make sure labels are in the back, or remove them using scissors. This strategy works best with T-shirts, socks, and underwear.

⭐ Enlist the help of your roommate.
Trade an item or skill you have for your roommate's wash-and-fold skills. Offer a party invitation you received, a hot prospect's phone number, or a short paper in exchange for an appropriate amount of laundry.

⭐ Wear less clothing.

The fewer clothes you wear, the fewer you'll need to wash. Skip unnecessary items like underwear and socks. Wear a long coat or sweater over bare skin.

⭐ Send clothes home.

Unless you have family members nearby, expect at least a week of turnaround time. You can save money by sending the clothes book-rate, but this method may take 10 days to 2 weeks.

Take your laundry through a car wash.

★ Hang clothes outside on a clothesline.
Put clothes outside on windy, rainy, or snowy days and let the weather do the work for you. Do not hang clothes outside on a very hot, sunny day. The heat of the sun can set the smell or stain and make the garment difficult to clean later on.

★ Shower with your clothes on.
Use a liquid soap, which will penetrate layers of clothing more effectively than bar soap. Rinse thoroughly. Alternatively, wear clothing in swimming pools and outdoor fountains, though chlorine may leave a residual odor.

★ Drive through a car wash with the windows open.
Pile clothes on the passenger seats of an open convertible or car with the windows open. Close your eyes and hold your breath.

HOW TO AVOID THE FRESHMAN FIFTEEN

⭐ Avoid foods you can eat with your hands.
Pizza, French fries, hamburgers, onion rings, bagels with cream cheese, hot wings, jalapeño poppers, dip
OKAY: Raw vegetables, fruit

⭐ Avoid foods you can get from a vendor at a sporting event.
Beer, peanuts, ice cream bars, nachos, popcorn, hot dogs, garlic fries
OKAY: Bottles of water, Popsicles

⭐ Avoid foods you can get from a vending machine.
Potato chips, soda, candy bars, cheese and crackers, cookies, muffins, hot chocolate
OKAY: Sugarless gum, diet soda, water, mini pretzels, black coffee

⭐ Avoid foods that melt quickly.
Ice cream, sorbet, gelato, ice cream bars, frozen custard, chocolate bars
OKAY: Fat-free frozen yogurt, Popsicles, fruit and juice bars, ice cubes

⭐ Avoid foods that you can eat with chopsticks.
Chinese stir-fry in heavy sauce, pad Thai, fried rice, chicken teriyaki, dim sum
OKAY: Sushi, steamed vegetables, brown rice, *be bim bop, pho*

⭐ Avoid foods that come in a crinkly bag.
Potato chips, cookies, tortilla chips, crackers, cheese puffs, nuts, snack cakes
Okay: Ready-to-eat salads (no dressing), cereal, rice, precut vegetables

⭐ Avoid foods that are orange.
Candied yams, pumpkin pie, cheddar cheese
Okay: Bell peppers, acorn squash, oranges, sweet potatoes (baked)

⭐ Avoid foods with phosphates.
Bacon, hot dogs
Okay: None

Be Aware
Trying to keep track of the number of calories in the foods you eat is difficult, impractical, and annoying. Think of the calorie content of food in terms of its equivalent in mugs of beer and adjust your intake accordingly (see chart on next page).

Food Equivalency Chart

Food item	Calorie equivalent in mugs of beer*
Apple pie, 1 slice	🍺🍺🍺🍸
Bagel with cream cheese	🍺🍺
Beef jerky, 1 stick	🍸
Breadsticks with marinara sauce, 6	🍺🍺🍸
Brownie, frosted	🍺
Burrito, bean and cheese	🍺🍺🍸
Cheeseburger	🍺🍺🍺🍸
Chicken breast, fried	🍺🍺🍸
Chicken fingers, 6	🍺🍺🍺
Chili, 1 cup	🍺🍺
Chocolate chip cookies, 10	🍺🍺🍺🍺🍺
Coffee with 2 tbsp. cream	🍸
Cola, 12-oz can	🍺
Dip, French onion, ¼ cup	🍺
Double bacon cheeseburger	🍺🍺🍺🍺
Doughnut, glazed	🍺🍸
Eggs Benedict	🍺🍺🍺🍺🍺🍺
Falafel in pita with yogurt dressing	🍺🍺🍺🍸
French fries, medium size	🍺🍺🍸
Fried-egg bagel sandwich, bacon and cheese	🍺🍺🍺🍺
Fried rice, vegetarian	🍺🍺🍸
Frozen yogurt, chocolate, ½ cup	🍺
Hot fudge sundae, small	🍺🍺
Hot wings, 8	🍺🍺🍺🍺
Hummus and pita bread	🍺🍺🍸
Latte, low-fat	🍺
Macaroni and cheese, 1 cup	🍺🍸
Milkshake, chocolate, 10 oz	🍺🍺🍸
Muffin, blueberry, large	🍺🍺🍺
Nachos, 8	🍺🍺
Pad Thai with chicken and shrimp	🍺🍺🍸
Pho	🍺🍺
Pizza, pepperoni slice	🍺🍺🍺
Popcorn, microwave popped, ½ bag	🍺🍸

Potato, baked, plain ....

Potato chips, 6-oz bag ....

Ramen noodles, 1 package ....

Salad dressing, balsamic vinaigrette, ¼ cup ....

Salad dressing, ranch, ¼ cup ....

Sandwich, corned beef on rye ....

Sandwich, peanut butter and jelly ....

Sesame chicken...

Spaghetti with meatballs..

Sugary breakfast cereal, 1 bowl, no milk ....

Taco, beef ....

Cocktails

Beer, light, mug ....

Bloody Mary..

Cosmopolitan ....

Daiquiri...

Fuzzy navel...

Gin and Tonic ....

Grain alcohol, shot...

Kamikaze..

Long Island iced tea ....

Malt liquor, 40 oz..

Margarita..

Martini ....

Mudslide...

Piña colada..

Rum, shot..

Rum and Coke..

Screwdriver ....

Seabreeze...

Sex on the beach..

Tequila, shot..

Vodka, shot ....

Whiskey, shot..

Whiskey sour...

Wine, glass ....

Wine cooler...

* One mug of beer is equivalent to 150 calories.

how to avoid the freshman fifteen

HOW TO PUT OUT A MICROWAVE FIRE

1 Turn off the microwave.
Press the STOP button. Do not open the door, or you will risk adding oxygen to the fire. Check for flames or smoke by looking through the glass window in the oven's door.

2 Unplug the microwave from the wall.
Do not yank on the cord. Wiggle the plug free at the wall.

3 Open the windows.
Smoke will escape the microwave through the vent. Open the windows to clear the smoke, and turn on a fan facing out of your room to blow the smoke through. Close the door to your room to keep the smoke from moving into the hallway and panicking your neighbors. If too much smoke collects in your room, you may set off the fire alarm.

4 Wait 30 seconds.
Microwaves are designed to contain a small fire without spreading heat or flames. Wait for the fire to burn itself out or use all available oxygen. If the fire does not go out on its own in half a minute, the seals on the microwave door may be old and allowing in oxygen to feed the flames. Call the fire department.

5 Use a fire extinguisher to douse the flames.

If a fire extinguisher rated type ABC is available, aim the nozzle at the base of the fire, and apply the P.A.S.S. technique to snuff out the flames: Pull the safety pin from the top of the extinguisher. Aim the nozzle at the base of the flames. Squeeze the handle of the extinguisher. Sweep the hose from side to side until the flames are out.

6 Check for flames.

If the fire has gone out, feel the glass door with the back of your hand. If it is hot to the touch, do not open it.

7 Wait another 30 seconds.

When the glass has cooled, open the microwave door. Step away from the microwave in case the newly introduced oxygen creates a flare-up.

8 Remove the burned item.

The container is likely to be hot. Use oven mitts or pot holders. Keep your face away from the container to reduce the possibility of steam burns.

9 Discard the food and container.

The container may have melted into the cooked item. Do not try to salvage the burned snack or its container. If it is still hot to the touch, place the burned item under running water before discarding.

Be Aware

Do not use the microwave again until it has been checked for damage.

HOW TO IDENTIFY UNSAFE CAFETERIA FOOD

Meat and Poultry

⭐ Check the color.
When fully cooked, beef turns brown or gray; chicken is white or brown without a trace of pink or red (depending on whether it is light or dark meat); and pork is also white, with no tinge of pink or red. If you cannot identify what kind of meat you are being served, do not eat it. No meat or poultry should ever be yellow, blue, or green.

⭐ Check the temperature.
Hot foods should be piping hot; cold foods should be chilled. If the temperature is in doubt, ask a food service operator for a cooking thermometer and stick it into the center of the item. Hot meats should be at least 145°F, cold foods no warmer than 40°F.

⭐ Poke with a fork.
If the juices run red, the meat is undercooked.

⭐ Look at the gravy.
Sauces and gravies may have a thick "skin" or float in a puddle of congealed oil. These items are a breeding ground for bacteria.

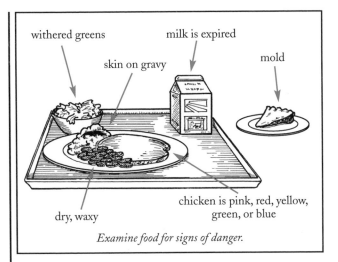

withered greens

milk is expired

skin on gravy

mold

dry, waxy

chicken is pink, red, yellow, green, or blue

Examine food for signs of danger.

Salad Bar

⭐ Look for a sneeze guard.
Salad bars and other self-serve areas should have plastic guards to protect food from germs. Avoid foods in areas without these protective devices.

⭐ Watch for slow food turnover.
Food left out too long will have a dry, waxy, or withered appearance. Food should not be left out from breakfast to lunch and lunch to dinner. If you suspect slow turnover, mark a piece of food with a carefully placed garnish; parsley works well. Return to the dining hall later in the day to see if your marked item is still present. If it is, complain to the chef or management.

how to identify unsafe cafeteria food

Avoid foods that need to be eaten soon after being cooked.

Scrambled eggs should not sit in a steam tray for more than two hours; hardboiled eggs keep at room temperature for two hours or for up to one week if refrigerated.

Packaged Foods

 Check the expiration date.

If it is past the date shown on the package, do not eat it. This applies to yogurt, milk, sushi, and any pre-pared or packaged foods.

 Check the package for damage.

If the seal is broken or the package looks damaged, do not eat the contents. Gently squeeze the bag of chips or pretzels to see if the bag holds air and remains firm. For vacuum-sealed jars, make sure the top has not popped up, which would indicate that the jar has been opened and the contents may be unsafe to eat. Do not eat food from dented cans—the sharp point of the dent may allow air and germs into the can.

Be Aware
- Watch for overripe fruits and vegetables.
  Extensive brown or black spots are not good.
- Check bread and pies for mold. Green means STOP.

HOW TO EAT WHEN YOU'RE BROKE

How to Eat for Nothing

⭐ Look for free samples.

Membership food clubs and grocery stores offer free food samples in their aisles. One or two sweeps through the store might supply you with a well-balanced meal, including a beverage. Weekends are the prime time for grocery store samples due to the high volume of shoppers. Travel the aisles with a partially filled cart for greater acceptance. Ice cream parlors usually allow you to sample a flavor or two.

⭐ Share your friends' bounty.

Monitor the campus mailroom for friends who receive care packages and ask them to share. Ask acquaintances on the college meal plan to bring you fruit and containers full of cereal. Follow pizza delivery people and ask the recipients for a slice after they've all taken their first piece. Promise to pay them back later.

⭐ Offer to deliver food (without a tip).

Many pizza restaurants offer a free pizza after every five (or some other number of) pizzas ordered. Collect the required number of orders from friends or dormmates, go to the pizza place, and pick up the pizzas—plus the free pizza. Be sure to collect payment for the pizzas in advance.

⭐ **Make friends at restaurants and bars.**
Making friends with cooks, waitstaff, or bartenders can result in free food, albeit leftovers at the end of a shift. Alternatively, offer to clear trays at a drive-in or restaurant. Consume leftover burgers, fries, and milkshakes between the table/car and kitchen.

⭐ **Participate in on-campus extracurricular activities.**
Join one or several university clubs that feature snacks at meetings and gatherings. Dorms offer special study nights during midterms and finals and frequently open their cafeterias for a study area. Snacks will be plentiful.

⭐ **Attend happy hour.**
Many bars and restaurants near campus serve complimentary hors d'oeuvres between 5 and 7 P.M.

⭐ **Sample the condiment bar.**
Some fast-food outlets have condiment bars with vegetables, sauces, salsa, and pickles. Help yourself to a few samples, but do not eat on the premises. Bring along a plastic bag to stow your snacks.

⭐ **Crash parties.**
Loiter at a local hotel and follow well-dressed people to trade shows, weddings, and bar mitzvahs. Visit the buffet table. Use caution when speaking to guests.

★ **Stake out hotel hallways.**
Snack on uneaten or partially eaten rolls, sandwiches, and garnishes from leftover room service trays. Make sure the meal has already been served and eaten, or you will risk a confrontation with a hungry hotel guest.

★ **Dumpster dive.**
The Dumpsters behind supermarkets and restaurants are almost always filled with untouched, uneaten food that was thrown away simply because it passed its expiration date. Take bread, canned goods, and other wrapped items. Do not break into a locked Dumpster.

How to Eat for Under a Dollar

★ **Eat fast food.**
Most fast-food restaurants have items on the menu that cost less than a dollar. Bulk up your sandwich with loads of condiments for extra calories; you will stay full longer.

★ **Look for specials and sales.**
Restaurants, convenience stores, and grocery stores all run sales and specials. Look for two-for-one deals on soda, candy, cookies, noodles, and soup, and for markdowns on perishables like meat, fruit, bread, and vegetables.

★ **Buy generic.**
Generic or store labels are always cheaper than name-brand items.

⭐ **Eat beans.**
Beans are a very cheap source of protein and fiber, and contain other essential nutrients.

⭐ **Eat pasta.**

⭐ **Eat a baked potato.**
A single potato usually costs less than a dollar and can be baked or heated in a microwave: Poke several fork holes in the potato to allow steam to escape and reduce the chance of explosion.

⭐ **Eat canned goods.**
Canned food is nearly always cheaper than its fresh alternative.

⭐ **Go for quantity, not quality.**
Buy foods that last for several meals so the average cost per meal is low. A loaf of bread will go a lot further than one piece of fruit. A jar of peanut butter might cost several dollars but will provide many meals for under a dollar when you pair it with two slices of bread and jelly packets from the cafeteria or a diner. Boxes of pasta, a package of bagels, generic cereal, a carton of eggs, oatmeal, a package of hot dogs, and cans of soup are cheap to begin with, and you will get more than one meal out of them.

HOW TO ASK YOUR PARENTS FOR MONEY

⭐ Focus on one parent.
Ask the parent you think is most likely to dole out funds. Hearken back to childhood by using the parent's favorite term of endearment, such as "Mommy" or "Pop."

⭐ Make the request in person.
Request money during a trip home. "Reluctantly" bring up the subject and look extremely embarrassed to be asking for a handout.

⭐ Write a letter if you are unable to ask in person.
Sending a plea for funds through the mail rather than telephoning or sending an e-mail will add a personal, serious, and traditional touch. Follow up with a phone call after the letter arrives. If you must make your request via e-mail, write your message in the form of a letter; start with a traditional greeting such as "Dear Mommy" and use proper punctuation and upper- and lowercase letters. Do not use abbreviations or emoticons. Be aware that it is easier for a parent to turn down a request by a reply e-mail than it is when responding by letter.

⭐ Tell a sob story.

Tell your parent that you have been trying to stand on your own two feet, but that college is much, much harder than you thought it would be, and that you are having to spend many hours a day in the library. Convey your concerns that getting a job will seriously impact your study time: Say that you could work a late-night job, but you're not sure how safe it is to be out alone in that neighborhood. This works especially well if you are taking a full course load. Detail your professors' difficult demands and your massive assignments.

⭐ Highlight your accomplishments.

Demonstrate what a solid investment you are. Point to your stellar grades, mention how you are juggling multiple commitments, list your extracurricular activities, and note any praise you've received from a professor. If you have not achieved any of these accomplishments, mention that you could achieve them if you had more time to devote to your studies and activities, and that money would facilitate getting that time.

⭐ Be specific about how much you need.

Request an exact amount and give the reason why you need the money. If you are direct, your parents will see your need as real and will be more likely to believe that you have explored other means of getting money. Your appeal is less compelling if you use a vague number or ask them to send what they can spare.

★ **Ask for more than you need.**
You will probably receive less than your requested amount, so overestimate the amount you need.

★ **Emphasize the intangible things the money will enable you to do.**
Funds might be needed to service your computer immediately, to take an off-campus course, or to cover membership fees for an organization that will look great on your résumé. If you tell them the money will go to buy furniture or a new printer, expect to show the items to them when they visit.

★ **Send a thank-you note.**
Express gratitude for and relief at the amount you receive. Your parents will be pleased with your good manners and will be more likely to send money again.

CHAPTER 3

EXTRACURRICULAR SURVIVAL SKILLS

HOW TO SURVIVE THE WALK OF SHAME

1 Locate all your belongings before vacating the premises.

2 Replace missing clothing.
If you are lacking pants, put your legs through the sleeves of your shirt and tape or staple the neck. If you are missing a shirt, use your socks as a bikini top, held in place with shoelaces from your running shoes: One lace goes through the top of each sock and is knotted at each end; that lace will go around your neck. The other lace goes through the heel of each sock, is knotted at each end, and becomes the strap that goes behind your back. Adjust for proper fit.

3 Dumb down your evening garments.
Remove any showy clothing or jewelry and wash your face to remove any trace of heavy makeup. Wear a hat, sunglasses, and drab clothing, if you have the option.

4 Avoid crowds.
Leave for home very early in the morning, when there will be fewer people on the street. If you wake up late, do not cross campus during peak class times.

5 | Walk briskly.
Match the gait of other passersby—but do not run. The faster you walk, the less likely you'll be noticed. Walking fast also cuts down on the amount of time and thus the number of people to whom you will be exposed.

Be Aware
- Arrange in advance a signal (bird call) to get your roommate's attention when you arrive after hours with no keys.
- Prepare and practice excuses and explanations for parents, boyfriend, and others you may encounter.

How to Avoid a Nightmare Hook-Up

1 | Do not get drunk.
When you need to refill your glass, do it yourself. Do not let a stranger get a drink for you. Drink a glass of water between alcoholic drinks.

2 | Clearly convey your desire for a straightforward hook-up.
Verbalize your desire to hook up with him for that night. State that you are not interested in pursuing a relationship of any sort. If he agrees to this, he may be interested in only a one-night stand as well, and may be just what you're looking for.

3 Clear the potential hook-up with a trusted friend.
Always go to a party or bar with a reasonably con-
scientious friend who does not have a penchant for
drink or proven bad taste in men. Leave your keys
with her. Introduce her to your potential hook-up and
ask if she thinks you are about to make a mistake.

4 Retrieve your keys from your friend.

5 Go to your place.
Your place is usually the preferred destination, since
you will be more in charge and comfortable.

6 Give yourself a last-minute excuse to get out.
Say that your roommates may be home and they
would create a problem, so you will have to say good-
night right now.

7 Assess his place.
If you do wind up at his apartment or dorm room,
look for signs of misrepresentation or personality dis-
order. Flip through recent photos to get an idea of his
social activities. Lock yourself in the bathroom and
check out the contents of his medicine cabinet. Check
the bedroom for concealed cameras. If his roommates
are home, note whether your hook-up is winking at
them or if he politely introduces you by name. Chat
with them to make sure you are comfortable in the
situation.

8 | End the encounter.

If you become uncomfortable or suspicious, leave quickly if you are at his place. If you are at home, say that you forgot that your boyfriend is coming over or that you've got a major headache/infection/test in the morning and need to get a few hours of sleep. If he seems reluctant to leave, give your roommate a sign to rescue you. Do not make any promises, however vague, to see him again.

Be Aware

• Going to your place for a hook-up can be problematic because he will know where you live and he may observe more about you than you would like. Also, you can't get up and leave when you want to end the hook-up.

• If you anticipate that you may be bringing a hook-up home, leave a note taped to your door. "Honey, I went to bed early. Please be quiet when you come in.—Mike." You can then explain later to your hook-up, if you want an excuse to end the evening, that your boyfriend has unexpectedly come over. If you want to continue with the hook-up, you can say that Mike is dating your roommate.

HOW TO DATE THREE PEOPLE AT ONCE

⭐ Assign them the same nickname.
Call them all "honey" or "sweetie" or "pumpkin" so that you do not accidentally use the wrong name with the wrong person. It also helps if you discuss the same topics and pick the same song as "our song."

⭐ Keep to a schedule.
See them only on their assigned day—Mary every Thursday, Emily every Friday, and Jenny every Saturday. They will see you as highly disciplined and will not expect to monopolize your time.

⭐ Select three different favorite bars, activities, or restaurants.
A special place for each reduces your chances of running into another date. Look for dimly lit, off-campus locations.

⭐ Be vague.
Provide few details to each date about your whereabouts during nondate evenings. Offer ambiguous responses like "I wish I had time to see you more often, too."

⭐ Keep your answering machine volume turned down.
If you are home with one of your dates and another calls, you will not be found out.

⭐ **Advise your roommate to say as little as possible.**
Explain your situation and ask for cooperation. Tell your roommate to say only "Nice to see you" when he sees one of your dates. He should avoid "Nice to meet you" or "Nice to see you again" since he may be easily confused about who he is talking to.

⭐ **Do not place photographs around your room.**
The fewer things and people to explain, the better. Also remove stuffed animals, flowers, cards, mix CDs, or anything that might look like a romantic gift.

⭐ **Tell everyone that you have a large family.**
Prepare for the time that you will be spotted with another date. If asked later who you were with, you can say she was your cousin.

⭐ **Refer to several part-time jobs.**
Say that you are sorry to be so unavailable because you are always working. Mention that you are saving all the money you are earning for tuition and other living expenditures so that you don't build expectations about gifts or expensive dates.

⭐ **Do not boast.**
Aside from your roommate, keep any mention of the simultaneous relationships to yourself. The more people you tell about your multiple assignations, the more likely it is that you will be discovered.

HOW TO SURVIVE SPORTS EMERGENCIES

MAN OVERBOARD

1 Stop rowing.
As soon as a team member falls off the scull, cease rowing.

2 Coordinate strokes.
Position the boat to within an oar's length of the victim.

3 Perform an extension rescue.
The person closest to the teammate in the water should extend an oar to the victim, making sure not to hit him with it. If the victim is injured or otherwise unable to grab the oar, the rescue must take place in the water; skip to step 7.

4 Pull the victim close to the boat.

5 Hold the victim against the side of the boat.
Do not attempt to bring him on board (or let him climb in), or you will risk capsizing the craft.

6 Row the boat to shore.

Stop rowing.

7 Enter the water.

Dive from the boat (or swim from shore) to the downed rower.

8 Approach the victim from the rear.

9 Perform a double armpit tow.

Facing the victim from behind, place your dominant arm under one of the victim's arms. Extend your arm across the victim's chest and grab him under the opposite armpit.

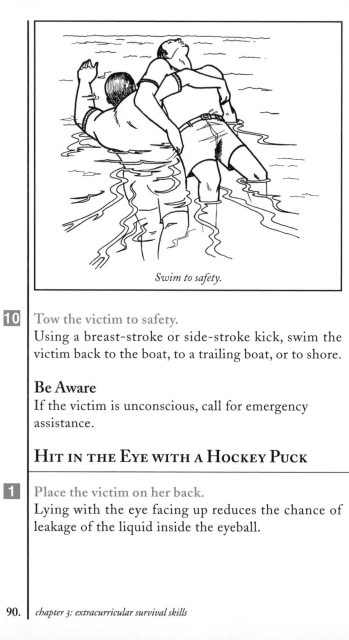
Swim to safety.

10 Tow the victim to safety.
Using a breast-stroke or side-stroke kick, swim the victim back to the boat, to a trailing boat, or to shore.

Be Aware
If the victim is unconscious, call for emergency assistance.

HIT IN THE EYE WITH A HOCKEY PUCK

1 Place the victim on her back.
Lying with the eye facing up reduces the chance of leakage of the liquid inside the eyeball.

2 | Elevate the head slightly.
Place a folded jacket or towel underneath the victim's head, elevating it slightly above the level of the heart to reduce pressure inside the skull and the eyeball.

3 | Apply a cold compress.
Place ice in a plastic bag. Do not apply the compress directly to the skin: Use a layer of clothing or plastic to prevent tissue from freezing. Hold the compress gently on the tissue surrounding the eye. Avoid pushing or putting pressure on the eye.

4 | Offer pain medication.
If the victim is conscious, administer 600 milligrams of ibuprofen. If ibuprofen is not available, use acetaminophen. Avoid administering aspirin: It may cause excess bleeding, which can be harmful during an eye operation.

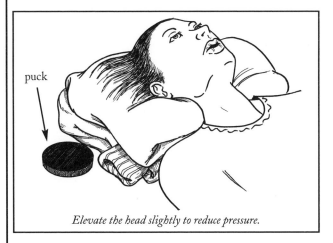

Elevate the head slightly to reduce pressure.

5 Get help.
Tell the emergency operator that you require an emergency room with a qualified ophthalmologist and ear-nose-throat (ENT) surgeon on call.

Be Aware
- A hockey puck to the head may fracture the socket containing the eye and/or rupture the eyeball itself. Both conditions require immediate medical attention.
- Always ask the victim about allergies to medicine before administering any drugs, even ibuprofen.

DART INJURY

1 If the dart is embedded in the head, neck, chest, or back, leave it in place.
Rinse a small, clean towel in cold water, wring it out, and wrap the towel around the base of the dart to stabilize it and prevent further penetrating or shearing injury. Take the person to the hospital, or call for an ambulance.

2 Remove the dart.
If the dart is embedded in an arm or leg, remove it from the victim using a fast, pulling motion. Put the dart in a safe location where it will not cause further injury. (If the dart bounced or has already fallen off the victim, ask where he was hit.)

3 Place the victim in a sitting position.

Locate the dart.

4 Examine the wound.

If blood is spurting from the wound, apply a clean cloth to the injury site. If there is bleeding but no spurting, skip to step 8.

5 Apply pressure.

Elevate the affected area above the level of the heart. Hold the cloth firmly in place for 5 minutes.

6 Remove the cloth and check the wound.

If blood continues to spurt, apply a new, clean cloth, elevate, and apply pressure for 15 additional minutes. Change the cloth as needed. For persistent oozing, apply pressure for 30 minutes.

7 Examine the wound.
Once the wound has stopped spurting, check the injury site, wiping away any seeping blood.

8 Rinse.
When the bleeding has stopped or slowed, gently rinse the wound under cool tap water.

9 Bandage.
Cover with a large, sterile dressing.

10 Clean the dart.
Rinse the dart under hot tap water, then wipe thoroughly with rubbing (isopropyl) alcohol.

11 Remove the victim from the field of play.

Be Aware

A tetanus booster may be required if the victim has not had one in the previous 10 years.

HOW TO SURVIVE A STADIUM RIOT

1 Scan the crowd.

Quickly determine the focus of the rioting: mascot, goalpost, star player, referee, fans, band members, coaches, or cheerleaders. Physically distance yourself as quickly as possible.

2 Hide any obvious school affiliation.

If the mob appears to be attacking your school's fans, remove any clothing items with school colors, letters, or emblems. Stuff these items into a nondescript bookbag or plastic bag. Wrap your arms around your bag and use it to shield your torso as you begin your escape. If you do not have an appropriate carryall, leave your school gear behind.

3 Create a protective helmet.

Stuff crumpled-up newspaper or cardboard inside your hat for cushioning. If you do not have a hat, place an empty popcorn tub or other container over your head.

4 Move away from the mascots.

Regardless of whether they are the focus of the riot, both teams' mascots are especially vulnerable to attack. Stay well clear of either mascot.

Move quickly away from the mascots.

5 Observe movement patterns.
Most rioters move en masse in a single direction toward a particular object. Determine which way the mob is headed.

6 Watch for projectiles.
Bend your knees and keep your head low to avoid flying cans, bottles, pennants, water balloons, rocks, pipes, benches, people, or other objects.

7 Move sideways through the crowd to the nearest exit.
Avoid moving forward (toward the center of the riot) or backward (against the surging mob).

Be Aware
If you're the cause of the riot due to your actions as a fan, player, or mascot, ditch your uniform or suit and run.

HOW TO GET
A FREE DRINK WHEN
YOU'RE BROKE

★ **Appeal to your friends' soft side.**
Tell your friends that you are having your annual "drink-free" night. When they look confused, express mild discomfort and then sheepishly admit you are broke. Your reluctance to take advantage of the situation may result in your friends plying you with free drinks.

★ **Goad strangers into making you drink.**
Sidle up next to someone, preferably from a boisterous state like Texas. Order water. When he ridicules you, tell him you have never had a drink before. Allow him to goad you into drinking for as long as he is willing to buy. This strategy will also work on someone who is alone and is not particularly attractive.

★ **Tell a sob story.**
Create a plausible tale of woe. Sit next to a woman with a sympathetic face. Say that you had to put your dog to sleep that day. Reveal that you caught your girlfriend in bed with your roommate. Pepper your story with as many details as possible. Cover your face with your hands. Apologize for being so upset and thank her for being such a good listener. Gratefully accept a drink.

⭐ Plan an accident.
Ask for a glass of water with a twist of lime. Pick a mark—choose someone with sweeping arm movements—and accidentally bump him with your elbow and spill your drink on yourself. When he offers to get you a new drink, ask for a gin and tonic. You can also set your glass of water near someone's elbow. When she knocks it over, allow her to replace it.

⭐ Scavenge leftover drinks.
Drink the half-empty beers or mixed drinks left behind by bargoers. Carry a small spray bottle of disinfectant or soapy water. Spray a napkin and wipe the glass with it. Beware of smokers who leave behind drinks—they often drop butts in their drinks or bottles.

⭐ Gamble.
Make bets that you know you will win, or perform a surefire bar trick for drinks. Select a mark, preferably someone who has been drinking heavily. You will need a small brandy snifter, an empty glass, and a stemless maraschino cherry.
- Place the snifter upside down over the cherry.
- Wager a free drink that you can get the cherry into the empty glass without touching the cherry or empty glass. The cherry can touch only the snifter, which must remain upside down. Squashing the cherry onto the rim is prohibited.
- When he bets, show him the power of centrifugal force. Hold the base of the snifter and rotate it quickly on the bar top. When the cherry starts

Rotate snifter.

Lift snifter off the table as the cherry spins.

Drop the cherry into the target glass.

spinning inside the glass, lift the snifter off the table. Keep rotating the snifter and hold it over the glass. When you slow your rotation, the cherry will drop into the glass. Collect your free drink.

Be Aware

- Frequent the same bar. Bartenders and waitstaff will get to know you and may occasionally send free drinks your way or let you drink on credit.
- Skip dinner. The drinks you do get will have more effect on an empty stomach.
- Frequent happy hours that have two-for-one specials. Other patrons may be willing to give you their "free" drink.

HOW TO OPEN A BOTTLE WITHOUT AN OPENER

Another Bottle

1 Hold the bottle you wish to open upright in your nondominant hand.

Grip the neck of the target bottle, placing your index finger over the back edge of the cap.

2 Hold the second bottle horizontally around the label.

Grip this bottle, the opener, as though shaking hands with the bottle.

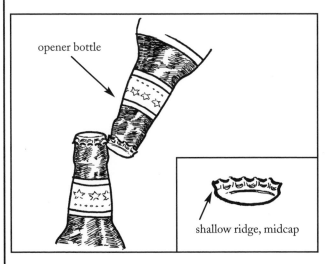

opener bottle

shallow ridge, midcap

3 Fit the shallow ridge found at midcap of the opener bottle under the bottom edge of the cap of the bottle you wish to open.

By using this ridge, and not the bottom of the cap, you will not risk opening the second bottle in step 4.

4 Using the opener bottle as a lever, press down and pry the cap off the target beer bottle.

5 Enjoy.

ALTERNATE METHOD:
Hold both bottles end to end perpendicular to the ground, with the crimped edges of the caps together, locking them in place. Pull. Be careful, however, as either or both bottle caps could come off.

LIGHTER

1 Grip the bottle in your nondominant hand.

Make a fist around the top of the bottle so that your thumb overlaps your index finger and the web between your thumb and index finger sits in the groove under the cap.

2 Fit the bottom of the lighter under the teeth of the cap.

Position the lighter so that it rests on the middle knuckle of your index finger.

3 Press the top of the lighter down and toward the bottle.

Use the index finger on your dominant hand to provide resistance.

4 Pry off the cap.

If necessary, turn the bottle and repeat.

TABLE EDGE

1 Put the teeth of the bottle cap against the edge of a table.

The cap should be on top of the table edge; the bottle should be below the table. Do not attempt on a soft wood or antique table.

2 Use your fist to hit the bottle.

The bottle will take a downward trajectory, and the cap will pop off.

Screwdriver, Spoon, Fork, or Knife

1 | Place the implement under the bottle cap, as high as it will go.

2 | Pry off the cap.
Slowly go around the cap and lift up each crimped area with the tool, similar to opening a can of paint.

3 | When the cap starts to move, fit the tool higher up under the cap and remove it.

Belt Buckle

1 | Unfasten your belt buckle. If your pants are in danger of falling down, sit.

2 | Pull the "tooth" of the buckle to one side.

3 | Fit the cap into the buckle so that one edge is wedged against the buckle.

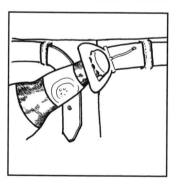

4 | Pry off.
Pull the bottle slowly. A quick tug may result in a spill.

5 | Refasten your belt.

Deadbolt Lock

1 Fit your bottle into the lock. Place the head of the bottle into the recession in a doorframe into which a deadbolt slips, so that the cap fits against the notch in the lock's frame.

2 Pull up slowly. The bottle cap should pop right off.

Fire Hydrant

1 Look for an arrow on top of the hydrant labeled "open."

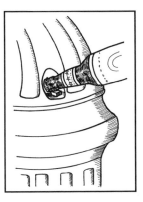

2 At the end of the arrow, locate the recess between the screw and the nut.

3 Insert the cap into the recess.

4 Press down slowly on the bottle until the cap comes off.

In-Line Skate

1 Place the cap between the shoe and the blade. Hold onto the bottle with your dominant hand. If you are wearing the skate, use the hand opposite the skate to open the bottle.

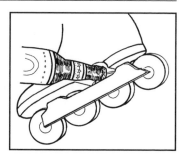

2 Pull up slowly on the bottle and pry off. Quickly right the bottle to avoid spilling.

Metal Pool Bridge

1 Hold the stick of the bridge in one hand and a beer bottle in the other. Do not attempt to open over the pool table.

2 Position the cap inside the opening of the bridge. Fit the cap snugly against the edge.

3 Press down on the bottle. Slowly increase the pressure until the cap loosens. Right the bottle immediately to prevent spillage.

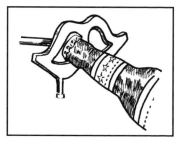

Vending Machine

1 Locate a newspaper, snack, or soda vending machine.
An older soda machine might actually have a bottle opener.

2 Place the cap in the coin return.
Wedge the cap against the top of the opening.

3 Press down slowly until the cap is removed.

Be Aware
Never drink from a bottle with broken or chipped glass.

HOW TO CHILL BEVERAGES WITHOUT A REFRIGERATOR

Indoors

⭐ Make your own cooler.
Fill a washing machine, bathtub, or sink with ice for an instant cooler. Drain the water when it warms and add more ice. For faster cooling, twirl the bottles in the ice. Guard these locations if they are in shared or public areas.

⭐ Use a toilet tank.
The water in the tank is usually cool. Place sealed bottles and cans in the tank. Thoroughly wash and rinse the bottle before drinking.

⭐ Use a soda machine.
Stick a bottle of wine up the ramp of a soda machine. Guard it well.

⭐ Use an aerosol "keyboard duster."
Turn the can upside down and spray it around the bottle from about six inches away. The cold air under pressure will come out more quickly, slightly chilling the beverage.

Hang bucket with beverages outside window.

Outdoors

⭐ Use the weather.

If the weather is cold, rainy, or snowy, place the beverages on your windowsill or hang a bucket or shelf from your window to store beverages outside. Do not leave drinks outside for more than an hour on very cold days, or you run the risk of freezing them. Do not hang drinks outside the window if you live on the first floor unless you are able to guard them constantly.

- **Bucket Method:** Tie a square knot to fasten one end of a rope to the handle of a bucket; secure the other end of the rope to your desk or another sturdy, immovable object. Dangle the bucket outside the window. Make sure the bucket is not overloaded, or the bucket or bottles may fall and seriously injure a passerby below. Do not fill the bucket with water; the cold air will cool the bottles enough.

- **SHELF METHOD:** Use a plank and knot a rope around each end. Lower the shelf out your window so that it is level and within arm's reach. Tie securely to sturdy objects inside the room. Place your bottles carefully on the shelf and hang it out the window. Note: Do not use this method on especially windy days.

⭐ Stow bottles and cans in a fountain.
Chilling your beverages in public places can result in theft or unwanted attention from authorities, so store your beverages in a less-trafficked location.

⭐ Ask an ice cream vendor to chill your bottle.
Ask a friendly looking vendor with an ice-cream or food cart to store your beverage in his cooler or refrigerator. Make sure you know his route if he moves around campus so you can retrieve it when it is needed. Do not entrust beverages to a vendor in a motorized vehicle.

HOW TO DEAL WITH "THE SPINS"

1 Focus your gaze on a stationary object in the room. Keep your eyes open. Avoid looking at ceiling fans. Stare at the object for one minute.

2 Close your eyes.

3 Picture the object you were looking at. Imagine that the object is imprinted on the inside of your eyelids.

4 Open your eyes. If the spinning returns, stare at your object for one minute.

5 Close your eyes. Repeat steps 3 and 4.

6 Repeat steps 3, 4, and 5 until the spinning stops or you pass out.

Be Aware

• The spins usually occur when your eyes are closed. Watch television, go out for some air, or eat a meal—anything to stay awake and keep your eyes open until you sober up.

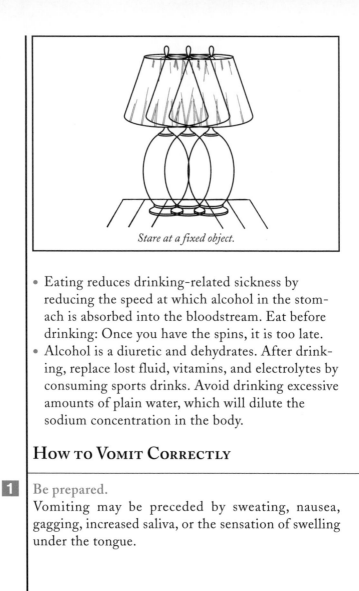

Stare at a fixed object.

- Eating reduces drinking-related sickness by reducing the speed at which alcohol in the stomach is absorbed into the bloodstream. Eat before drinking: Once you have the spins, it is too late.
- Alcohol is a diuretic and dehydrates. After drinking, replace lost fluid, vitamins, and electrolytes by consuming sports drinks. Avoid drinking excessive amounts of plain water, which will dilute the sodium concentration in the body.

How to Vomit Correctly

1 Be prepared.
Vomiting may be preceded by sweating, nausea, gagging, increased saliva, or the sensation of swelling under the tongue.

2 | Move quickly.
Get to a quiet bathroom or a private area with an appropriate receptacle, such as a toilet, trash can, or metal bowl. If outdoors, look for an area secluded by trees or bushes. Avoid public spaces.

3 | Remove necktie or necklace.

4 | Open collar.
Unbutton your shirt at least two buttons and pull the sides apart. If you are wearing a pullover, remove it completely, if time permits. Tie back long hair.

5 | Relax.
Do not resist.

6 | Target a destination.
Vomit into the receptacle. If vomiting into a toilet, grip the sides for support.

7 | Wait.
The first bout of vomiting may not be the last. Wait several minutes to make sure you remain in control.

8 | Clean up.
Wash your hands and face, rinse out your mouth, and brush your teeth.

9 | Return to the party.

HOW TO DEAL WITH THE AFTERMATH OF A WILD PARTY

HOLE IN THE WALL

1 Hide it.

If the hole is above waist height, hang a poster or other wall decoration over the hole. If the hole is below waist height, move a sofa or easy chair from another location and place it in front of the hole. Sweep or vacuum the floor where the furniture was previously located, or its absence will be obvious.

2 Make faux-Spackle.

Slowly mix flour and water together until they form a thick paste, or use white toothpaste for a quick fix.

3 Fill the hole.

Using a butter knife or your fingers, fill the hole with the mixture. For very large holes, first fill the cavity with crumpled newspaper. Make sure the paste completely covers the hole and extends onto the wall around it. Spread paste evenly and remove clumps.

4 Allow to dry.

Wait at least 30 minutes, or until the paste hardens.

before

after

how to deal with the aftermath of a wild party

5 Sand.
Using fine-grain sandpaper, sand the wall until it is smooth. Paint if necessary.

6 Camouflage the fix.
If the wall color was not white originally, use a suitable Magic Marker or nail polish to conceal your repair.

Be Aware
Repairing large broken sections (bigger than fist-size) may require extensive sawing of the cracked drywall and patching with drywall and/or chicken wire, which is a difficult, time-consuming process. For holes of this size, cover the affected area with a piece of furniture until professional repairs can be made or you move out.

Broken Window

1 Secure the remaining glass.
Stripe duct tape diagonally across pane to help prevent further breakage.

2 Patch the hole.
Use cardboard to cover the hole, securing it with more duct tape.

3 Pull down the shade or close the curtains.

Be Aware

- If you are expecting to have a particularly raucous party, striping windows with tape beforehand can minimize damage.
- Other things that can be fixed with duct tape include torn upholstery, plates and mugs (but do not put in dishwasher), pole lamps, putters, vases, end tables, and small goldfish bowls.

RED WINE SPILL

1 | Blot rug or carpet immediately.
Use an absorbent cloth (like an old T-shirt) to soak up as much of the stain as possible. Do not rub the stain, as you will push the wine further into the carpet.

2 | Saturate.
Pour large amounts of club soda or cold water on the stain and surrounding area. White wine is also an effective stain remover, but pouring good wine on the carpet is wasteful.

3 | Repeat.
Reiterate steps 1 and 2 several times until the stain disappears. If the stain remains but is no longer being transferred to the cloth, stop blotting and saturating.

4 | Make a stain removal paste.
If stain persists, make a paste of 3 tablespoons of borax or baking soda and 1 tablespoon of water.

5 | Rub the paste onto the stain.
Use an old toothbrush or a spoon. Allow the paste to dry.

6 | Vacuum.

7 | Repeat steps 4 through 6 until the stain is no longer visible.
If the stain still remains, treat with a commercial carpet spotter.

Wax on Carpet

1 | Allow to dry.
Do not attempt to remove the wax while it is still hot.

2 | Place an ice cube on the wax.
Hold the ice in place for 30 seconds or until the wax hardens completely.

3 | Break and scrape.
Gently break apart the wax with your fingers until you have a pile of loose shavings. Scrape as much wax as possible off the carpet with a spoon or dull knife.

4 | Vacuum.

5 | Iron.
If wax still remains, place a clean cloth or paper bag over the wax. Slowly move a warm iron across the cloth or bag. The wax will melt and adhere to the

warm surface of the cloth/bag. Rotate the cloth/bag
as the wax is absorbed so you are always ironing on a
clean section.

6 Vacuum.
If wax remains, use a commercial carpet cleaner to
remove remnants.

Spill on Keyboard

1 Unplug the keyboard.
Do not turn on the computer.

2 Place the keyboard upside down on an absorbent
cloth.

3 Leave overnight.

4 Dry.
Using a can of compressed air or a blow-dryer, thoroughly dry keyboard, making sure no wet or damp
areas remain.

5 Test.
Plug the keyboard into an older computer or one
without critical files, if available. Turn on the computer. If the keyboard is recognized and the computer
works properly, it is safe to plug the keyboard into
your main system.

Be Aware

- Powering up a computer with a wet keyboard can result in an electrical short circuit, which damages the entire system.
- For laptop computers, keep the system off and follow steps 2 through 5. If you are not sure the keyboard is completely dry, send the unit out for repair before turning it on.
- Highly acidic drinks like coffee and tea or sugary beverages like hot chocolate and soda may cause electrical parts to corrode if the spill is not properly cleaned.

HOW TO SURVIVE INITIATION NIGHT

SWALLOWING SOMETHING GROSS

1 Control your breathing.
Take deep breaths and exhale slowly. Ignore others who are attempting to eat the item, especially if they are gagging or vomiting. Remember, it will go down in a second.

2 Center yourself.
Visualize yourself lying on a beach, sipping a cool drink, or strolling by a breezy lake.

3 Numb your tongue.
Apply ice or an over-the-counter oral numbing agent to your tongue. You will temporarily lose feeling but not your sense of taste.

4 Breathe through your mouth.
You can reduce any bad taste by breathing through your mouth, not your nose.

5 Move the object to the back of your tongue.
Taste buds on the front and sides of the tongue are most sensitive. Quickly push the object as far back on your tongue as you can.

6 | Swallow.
Use one quick gulp. Do not chew.

GETTING PADDLED

1 | Wear several pairs of underwear.
Underwear will reduce pain if you are required to lower your pants. Consider wearing flannel boxers. Avoid thongs.

2 | Wear thick pants.
Put on bulky trousers, not shorts. Avoid corduroy, which may leave paddle lines.

3 | Do not bend all the way forward.
Bending fully forward will tightly stretch your gluteus maximus, creating a less-forgiving surface and reducing your body's natural padding. Try to remain upright, or bend only slightly.

4 | Exhale.
Inhale deeply, then exhale as the paddle connects.

ENDURING PSYCHOLOGICAL TORTURE

1 | Do not show weakness.
Your tormentors will look for weak individuals, focus on them, and exploit their fears. Resist the urge to burst into tears, beg for mercy, flee, or bond with your tormentors.

*Be prepared
to swallow anything.*

*Wear several pairs
of underwear.*

Visualize yourself in a pleasant environment.

2 | Live in the moment.

Do not worry about what comes next. Do not dwell on what just passed. Deal with each horror on its own terms, as it happens.

3 | Keep your mind occupied.

You may be isolated from the group, kept awake for several days, or seemingly singled out for special treatment. In such situations, keep your brain active by recalling the lyrics of all the songs you know, remembering pleasurable experiences, or focusing on the goal of joining the group.

HOW TO SURVIVE A NIGHT IN JAIL

1 Request a single.

If you notice an empty cell, ask to be housed there. Do not offer special reasons for wanting a private cell—those factors may work against you if you are later placed in a group cell.

2 Do not show fear.

Fear means weakness in jail. If you cannot stop shaking, pretend you are psychologically unsound: Wave your arms around, babble nonsense, and yell at no one in particular.

Relax hand and roll finger to make a clean print.

3 | Stay within sight of the guard.
The cell may be monitored in person by a guard or via closed-circuit television. Make sure you remain visible.

4 | Do not sleep.
Lying down on a bench or cot gives other inmates the opportunity to claim that you are lying on "their" bunk. Sit on the floor with your back to the wall, preferably in a corner of the cell. Do not remove any clothing to use as a blanket or pillow, or you will risk losing the item to other inmates.

5 | Keep to yourself.
Do not start a conversation with anyone, but do not be rude. Answer any questions you are asked, and keep your responses short. Do not talk about the reason for your arrest, as there may be police informants in the cell. Do not make eye contact with other inmates, but do not avert your eyes.

6 | Do not accept favors.
Other inmates may offer to help you in various ways, then claim that you "owe" them. Resist the temptation to ask for or accept help.

7 | Do not tell anyone you are a college student.
The population of the cell may make various assumptions about the privileges, wealth, health, preferences, defenselessness, connections, and value of students.

8 | Do not try to escape.

CHAPTER 4

CLASS SURVIVAL

HOW TO SURVIVE WHEN YOU'RE CALLED ON AND DON'T KNOW THE ANSWER

⭐ **Stall for time.**
Repeat the question aloud. Very slowly, say, "So [deep breath], essentially [deep breath], what you are [clear throat] asking me is . . ." This will buy you a few extra seconds to create a suitable response.

⭐ **Redirect.**
If you've done the reading but simply don't know a particular answer, steer the subject to a more familiar topic. Say, "That's an interesting question that leads me to the essential part of last night's reading . . ."

⭐ **Discuss another subject.**
Answer confidently. Act like you are convinced that you know the right answer. Make eye contact with the professor as you expound on the topic of your choice.

⭐ **Quote the book.**
Flip open the book and begin to scan the pages. Say, "I really couldn't say this any better than the author— I remember a quote in here somewhere; give me a moment to find it. . . ." After a silent moment or two,

the professor will move on to another student. Have a passage ready to read in case the professor returns to you for your answer.

⭐ Feign choking.
Begin coughing vigorously and point to your mouth. Wheeze for greater effect. After a few seconds of a coughing fit, say you need to leave to get a drink of water. Come back only when you are sure the topic has changed.

⭐ Be honest.
Since some professors appreciate honesty, consider admitting that you do not know the answer, but be prepared for an embarrassing public rebuke.

Be Aware
- If you are not prepared for class, do not wear a big floppy hat, dress in bright colors, or do anything to draw the professor's eye. Do not make eye contact with the professor. If possible, sit behind a tall student to help conceal your presence.
- Read the introduction and conclusion of an assignment to gain enough basic information to bluff your way through an unexpected question.

how to survive when you're called on and don't know the answer

HOW TO WRITE A LAST-MINUTE PAPER

⭐ Reduce, reuse, and recycle.
Reduce your study time, reuse old texts, and recycle old ideas. Select a topic or thesis that you have written on before in a different class. You already know the material, and you can lift particularly strong points or written passages.

⭐ Write an outline.
Figure out your main thesis and write down all the points you will use to support your main idea. Refer to this while you are writing your paper; it will help you stay on theme and maximize your time.

⭐ Know your professor.
Make your essay fit a professor's personality or agenda. Do not write on a topic in which she is a specialist. She will see the flaws or shortcomings in your argument immediately.

⭐ Focus on what you know.
Write on an issue about which you are passionate. You will write more quickly and easily and in a persuasive and compelling manner.

⭐ Manipulate the formatting.
Increase the leading (the space between each line of text), point size (the size of the type), and margins.

Select a font that is large to begin with. These visual tools will make your essay look longer. Do not go overboard: Using 18-point type is an immediate give-away that you are fudging the length of the paper.

Be Aware

Take interrelated courses or a general and a specific course on the same subject. If you have taken a Shakespeare class, take an Elizabethan history course. This will cut down on studying multiple material.

How to Cram for a Test

⭐ Pull in outside material.
Read condensed or simplified versions of the course material. Dig up old textbooks or material from previous classes. Take advantage of study guides, whether published online or photocopied from previous classes. If you are in an English class, watch the movie adaptation of a required book or play. Check the description of a work on literary websites.

⭐ Skim reading material.
Read the first and last sentence of paragraphs. Read the book jacket, introduction, conclusion, table of contents, and glossary.

⭐ Seek out other students.
Ask someone from class if you can photocopy his notes. Also ask what he considers the main points to

study. If he's been paying attention in class, he will have a good idea of what will be on the exam.

⭐ **Review exams from previous courses taught by your professor.**
Check your campus and dorm libraries; they often keep old exam files on hand.

⭐ **Find a quiet place to study.**
Seek out a well-lit empty classroom, coffee shop, or quiet area of the library. Avoid studying in your dorm room or apartment; there are too many distractions. If you can find a friend to study with, bring him along. You can quiz each other periodically and keep each other's spirits up. Bring caffeinated drinks, snacks, gum, and anything else you might need to stay alert. You do not want to be distracted by hunger.

⭐ **Maintain your normal routine.**
If you normally eat breakfast, eat something before the exam. Practice "state-dependent" learning—if you drink coffee while studying, drink coffee during or right before your exam. If you chew gum while memorizing slides, chew gum during a test.

⭐ **Be prepared.**
Wear comfortable clothes in layers in the event that the lecture hall or classroom is too hot or cold. You do not want your external surroundings to distract you. If you work better in complete silence, bring earplugs. Bring extra pens, pencils, and blue books.

★ Use every minute before your test.

Review your notes or texts up to the moment your exam begins. Information you most recently reviewed will be uppermost in your mind during the exam; this is called the "recency effect." You are likely to recall specific details that you can effectively incorporate in an essay.

★ Do not discuss the subject as you enter the examination room.

Last-minute discussions about content or people's panicked questions can be confusing and misleading. You've done all you can—stay focused.

HOW TO SLEEP IN THE LIBRARY

⭐ Find the right location.
Look for a spot that is not heavily trafficked. Well-heated, dimly lit rooms with small cubicles or carrels near deserted stacks are ideal locations.

⭐ Sleep on the desk.
Spread a long coat or blanket, yoga mat, or crumpled-up newspaper on the desk to cushion the surface. Ball up a sweater or sweatshirt to use as a pillow. Assume the fetal position and tuck yourself into the space.

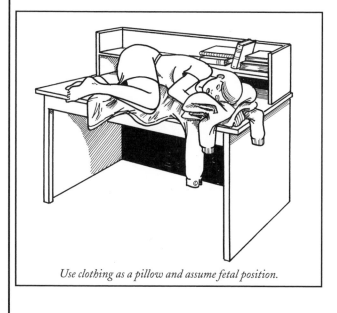

Use clothing as a pillow and assume fetal position.

Build a sleepchamber.

⭐ Build a sleepchamber under a carrel.
Drape coats, sweatshirts, and sweaters over the desk to block the view and the light. Crawl under the desk, taking water, snacks, a small pillow, and other provisions. Create a wall around you by piling up books. Set an alarm clock if you have a class or meeting later in the day.

⭐ Create a bed out of chairs.
Put two chairs together. Lay fabric or paper between your skin and the chairs' vinyl or wooden seats; the seat of a chair is a breeding ground for microbes.

Be Aware

- Protect your belongings. Conceal your wallet on your person. Leave your laptop at home.
- To avoid getting stiff, regularly stretch your legs and arms when you awaken. Roll onto your back and raise your arms and legs toward the ceiling. Flex and point your feet several times. Repeatedly bend your knees and straighten your legs. Shake out your arms. Shift position by rolling on your back to your other side, keeping legs bent.

How to Hook Up in the Library

1 Scout out a suitable makeout location.

Look for dim lighting and empty aisles in the stacks on a higher floor. Avoid areas near doors, entrances, main aisles, and passenger elevators. Library carrels, stairwells, and freight elevators in out-of-the-way locations are also good options. The oversized book collection features large tables and big, bulky volumes that allow for privacy. Determine less-traveled areas by reviewing the Dewey Decimal System. Sections that begin with the call numbers below are most likely to be quiet:

> 090 Manuscripts and book rarities
> 110 Metaphysics
> 170 Ethics (moral philosophy)
> 210 Natural religion
> 480 Hellenic; Classic Greek
> 510 Mathematics
> 670 Manufactures

707 Antiques and collectibles
930 General history of the ancient world

Sections with the following call numbers offer more risky locations but may provide some inspiration and atmosphere for the hook-up:

440 Romance languages, French
577 Pure science: General nature of life
618 Gynecology and other medical specialties
757 Painting: Human figures and their parts
770 Photography and photographs
811 Poetry

2 Time your rendezvous.
Select a time when your designated location will be deserted.

3 Meet at a predetermined location.
Pass a note to your hook-up target with a time and location. Indicate a specific Dewey Decimal section for the rendezvous.

Be Aware
Be respectful of the books. Do not damage or misuse them.

HOW TO PULL AN ALL-NIGHTER

⭐ **Eat a light dinner.**
Do not skip a meal, but do not eat to the point of drowsiness or sluggishness. Select foods with protein, like chicken breast, and complex carbohydrates, such as whole-wheat bread, brown rice, or beans, to provide you with energy and stamina for a long night. Later, when you feel your energy ebb, eat an energy bar.

⭐ **Consume peppermint.**
Peppermint is a stimulant; even a whiff of it will make you more alert and awake. Eat peppermint candy, chew peppermint gum, or drink peppermint-flavored herbal tea. Rub peppermint oil on your temples or wrists.

⭐ **Turn on the radio or television.**
A bit of white noise in the background will engage your senses. Select a classical or jazz station on the radio. If you turn on the television, turn to an infomercial or shopping channel. Keep the volume low. Do not select a rerun of your favorite situation comedy or anything you might otherwise be interested in.

⭐ **Turn on a strong overhead light.**
A bright light will help you see what you are reading as well as prevent you from falling into a deep sleep.

Close the curtains and put clocks out of sight; your body will become confused as to what time of night it is.

⭐ Turn down the thermostat.
The cold temperature will help keep you awake. Make sure the temperature does not dip below 50°F, at which you are susceptible to hypothermia, especially if you have wet hair or skin. A high temperature slows your pulse and makes you drowsy.

⭐ Do not lie down.
Pinch yourself or wear tight shoes and constricting underwear. Physical discomfort will keep you distracted and awake.

⭐ Consume caffeine.
Drink caffeinated beverages or eat a few caffeinated mints, but proceed with caution: Too much caffeine can leave you distracted and wired. Three hundred milligrams is considered a safe daily amount of caffeine for adults, which translates into a six-pack of soda or three to four cups of brewed coffee.

⭐ Breathe deeply.
Go to an open window or step outside for a few minutes. Stand up straight, close your eyes, and inhale deeply through your nose. Hold the breath for as long as you can. Exhale slowly through your nose or mouth. Repeat several times. Deep breathing will clear your mind and give you a shot of energy.

Stretch.

Stretch your limbs by taking a walk or doing a few yoga poses. This will work out any tension you are holding in your muscles.

- Lift your arms over your head and reach for the sky, alternating arms.
- Lean over to each side and then lean forward from the waist, bringing your arms out in front of you and down to the ground.
- Let your arms dangle; swing them from side to side.

 Do a headstand.

Increase your circulation by standing on your head.

- Find an area of clear floor space next to a wall.
- Kneel on the floor, facing the wall.
- Place your head on the floor a few inches from the wall.
- Place your forearms on the floor on either side of your head.
- Raise your body and legs slowly up the wall. Keep your body weight on your arms, not your head. Lean against the wall as needed.

 Raise your heart rate.

If you find yourself nodding off, do a few calisthenics to raise your heart rate. Do 25 jumping jacks, or skip rope or jog in place for 5 minutes.

 Get a study partner.

Even if he is not cramming for the same exam, you and your partner can quiz each other and talk as

Standing on your head will increase circulation.

you start to get drowsy. Do not stay up with someone you know will distract you with either idle chatter or sexual tension.

Be Aware

Even if you don't plan on going to sleep, set your alarm clock. To make sure that you are awake when you need to be, set every alarm you can find—watches, computers, cell phones, and hand-held electronic devices often have built-in alarms. Arrange for a friend or your roommate to back up the alarms with a wake-up call.

HOW TO TAKE A TEST WHEN YOU HAVE NOT STUDIED

Essay

⭐ Find a pocket of related knowledge.
Pull in details from a subject you know well. If you are passionate about abstract expressionism, bring in details of the art movement to answer a question in a twentieth-century history exam.

⭐ Use a few key words.
Employ short, less common words, such as *wan, fey, nay,* and *cur.* Add a few French bons mots. If you cannot spell the words, write sloppily. You will impress your professor with your linguistic erudition, which is better than not impressing him at all.

⭐ Write something.
Do not leave a question unanswered. You may not receive full credit for the answer, but displaying some knowledge about something will prevent you from taking a zero.

⭐ Scribble an outline.
On the inside cover of your blue book, illegibly write what appears to be an outline of an answer to show that you thoughtfully planned your answer.

★ Do not complete the last sentence.
No matter when you finish the essay exam, do not write the last sentence. Instead, write "TIME" across the bottom of your exam. This indicates that you would have written much more if you had more time.

Multiple Choice

★ Eliminate the wrong answers immediately.
When there are four choices, two answers are usually completely wrong. Cross them out. If you can discount any other answer, cross it out. "None of the above" and "all of the above" are often the correct answer. Do not discount these right away if you are unsure of the answer.

★ Trust your instincts.
Do not talk yourself out of your gut reaction. If you think a particular choice is the right answer, there is a reason. You may vaguely recall a lecture, something you read in passing, or even relevant information from an episode of your favorite television show.

★ Look for a pattern on your answer sheet.
Watch for some order, be it ABCDABCDABCD or BADDABBADDAB. Be wary if your answers are AAAAAAAAAAAA.

★ Do not labor over one question.
All questions are worth the same amount on multiple-choice exams, so do not get overly involved in any one

question. Move on and return to unanswered questions as you have time.

⭐ Answer every question.
Very seldom are wrong answers weighted more heavily against you than an unanswered question. Depending on the number of choices, you have a 20 to 25 percent chance of answering a question correctly. Guess every time.

Be Aware
- Take a class pass/fail if it is not in your concentration, if you have an overloaded schedule, or if you are concerned about your grade point average.
- There are usually more "true" answers than "false" answers on a true/false exam because false answers are harder to write.
- Determine what part of the test counts for the most points. Spend a proportionate amount of your time on this section.
- When possible, reuse facts and information from the multiple-choice portion of an exam in an essay question.

How to Postpone an Exam or Get an Extension for a Paper

⭐ Blame another class/professor.
Explain that you had another exam right before the one you want to reschedule, and that since the professor was nice enough to let you run over the allotted

time to finish, now you don't have enough time to take this exam.

⭐ Blame stress.
Explain to the professor that you care so much about the test/paper that you're paralyzed and unable to concentrate. Bring in problems from other areas of your life, and talk about how everything is coming down on you all at once. Say that you are afraid the stress is becoming too much to handle.

⭐ Blame your alarm clock.
Say you were studying all night and slept through your alarm. Offer to meet the professor in person to demonstrate your understanding of the material. Schedule the meeting for several days hence.

⭐ Blame your computer.
Leave your professor a voicemail in the middle of the night and explain in a panicked voice that your computer crashed and you've lost the file. Say that you are starting over from scratch on a friend's computer and that you will deliver the paper as soon as possible. Make sure that you call the professor's office number rather than her home phone number—you are unlikely to gain the empathy you're looking for if you wake your professor in the middle of the night.

⭐ Send an unreadable file.
Contact your professor five minutes before the paper is due. Say you are having trouble printing. Ask for a

how to take a test when you have not studied

Extension Strategies

Blame your alarm.

Blame an accident.

Cry.

Blame your computer.

Blame your pet.

Cry.

short extension. Be prepared for your professor to suggest that you e-mail her the paper or put it on a disk and take it to her office to print. If this occurs, send the wrong file or send a system file that cannot be opened. In the text of the e-mail, promise to drop off a hard copy as soon as you are able to print the file, and be sure to take a hard copy as soon as you are finished writing it.

★ Collapse.
Attend the exam as expected, but after sitting with the test for about five minutes, interrupt the class with a disruptive sickness. Vomiting, fainting, or a seizure are popular choices. The professor will have little choice but to allow you to reschedule the exam. Offer your apologies and say that you would continue with the test if you could.

★ Cry.

how to take a test when you have not studied

HOW TO SURVIVE A BORING CLASS

⭐ Pull your hair or pinch yourself.
Making yourself physically uncomfortable will make you less likely to fall asleep.

⭐ Wear as few items of clothing as possible.
The cold will keep you awake.

⭐ Hide more interesting reading material.
Prop open your textbook and conceal a novel or magazine inside it. Hold a highlighter in your hand and pretend to be taking notes as you read.

⭐ Suggest holding class outside.
If the weather is nice, ask the professor to teach out on the college green. This strategy rarely works for large survey classes or the sciences.

⭐ Send text messages on your cell phone.
Engage in a running text message exchange with other students in the class about how bad the professor is. Make sure that your keypad is set to mute so that you do not distract other students around you or draw your professor's attention to yourself.

⭐ Make paper airplanes.
Make as many models as you can. Pretend they are having fierce battles.

Paper Airplane

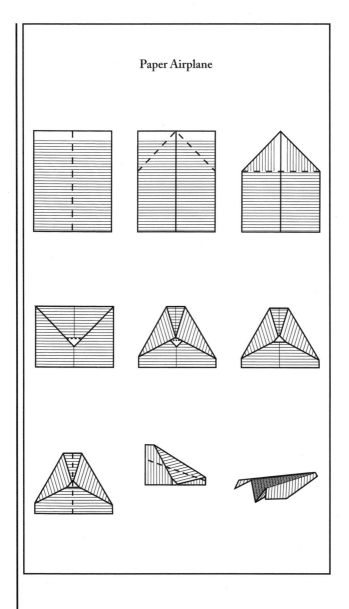

★ **Keep a list of words with dirty meanings.**
Write down words with alternate sexual meanings *(melons, stock, position, score)* as they are spoken by your professor. In the right frame of mind, almost any word will work.

★ **Take notes with your nondominant hand.**
Concentrate on staying in the lines.

★ **Take notes in a foreign language.**
Practice your language skills by translating your professor's lecture. Bring along your translation dictionary to increase your vocabulary.

★ **Keep a superlative log.**
Identify the most interesting people in the class on a daily basis. Observe how people change over time. Categories could include:
• Most attractive
• Tallest
• Blondest
• Ugliest
• Dirtiest
• Dumbest

★ **Pretend you are a secret agent.**
You are on a dangerous mission and must make it through the class alive. Spy on people to see what they are writing. Use a small hand mirror and a penlight to send Morse code to a confederate across the room.

How to Sleep in Class

1 Wear a hat.

Sharply bend the brim of a baseball cap and pull the visor low over your face to hide your eyes in the shadow. Do not wear a wool ski hat, beanie, or yarmulke, as none of these casts a shadow.

2 Sit in the rear of the class.

Choose a seat in the back of the classroom or at least far enough from your professor that he will not notice your heavy breathing.

3 Sit behind a tall person.

Position yourself behind a member of the basketball or volleyball team to interrupt your professor's line of vision. Sitting behind an obese person can also block your professor's sight line.

4 Sit on the opposite side of the class from known class participants.

5 Pad the desktop in front of you.

Fold a scarf, sweater, or sweatshirt on your desk. Bend one arm and place your elbow on the folded item.

6 Assume the napping position.

- Place your thumb under your chin, supporting your jaw.
- Rest your four fingers on the side of your face.
- Balance your head on your hand, keeping it upright.
- Place your notebook open and in front of you; hold a pen in your other hand, to look as if you are ready to take notes.

Be Aware

- Avoid wearing dark sunglasses in class. While they may serve to shade your eyes, they also attract attention.
- Do not let your head slump down to your chest.
- Do not rest your head on your desk.
- Do not lie down.

HOW TO GET INTO A CLASS THAT IS FULL

⭐ Befriend someone in the registrar's office.
An inside contact can place you at the top of a wait-list, determine the likelihood of getting into a particular class, give you information about the professor, or even slip you statistics on the dropout rate of the class.

⭐ Ask the professor in person.
Make the extra effort to plead your case directly. Seek out the professor during her office hours before the first class.

⭐ Present a compelling reason.
Earnestly convey a specific reason as to why you are so keen on taking this particular class. Mention that you've already done a lot of work in the area of study, refer to an obscure article, or say that you've published articles on the subject. Convince the professor that your experience and enthusiasm will make the class better for all the students.

★ Flatter the professor's curriculum vitae.
Bring up a few details about the professor's alma mater, publications, academic expertise, and reputation. Demonstrate that you are an admirer who wants to study at the feet of the master.

★ Attend the first class.
See if someone drops it or if there are unexpected openings. Stay for the whole class, and participate. Make your presence known. Have all necessary paperwork on hand in case the professor agrees to admit you to the class.

★ Be persistent.
Go to the professor's office. Leave her numerous voicemail messages. Visit her office again. Keep yourself in her field of vision—she may give in and admit you just so that you will leave her alone.

★ Cry.
Crying may help you gain sympathy.

★ Convince a student to drop the class.
Explain why the class is so important to you. Offer goods and services, or perhaps some money for her trouble. Avoid direct threats.

HOW TO SURVIVE CLASS WHEN HUNGOVER

 Stay up.
Rather than sleep off your drinking binge, stay awake through the night: You will be wired with exhaustion by the time you get to class. Stay out for the night, winding up at a greasy spoon.

 Medicate.
In the morning, take a combination vitamin B and C pill or an antihistamine with a stimulant. Dab hemorrhoid cream under your eyes to reduce puffiness. Drink lots of water. Carry a bottle of water with you.

 Eat breakfast.

 Enjoy the hair of the dog.
Drink a beer or knock back a shot before you go to class. You'll retain your buzz and delay your hangover until the class is over. Take care not to act the fool.

 Drink an energy drink.
For added pep, consume a sports drink.

 Wear a hat.
A hat with a brim will shield your eyes from harsh lighting and can serve as a cover should you fall asleep.

⭐ **Show up on time.**
Walking in late will only draw attention to you and your condition. If you do arrive late, wait until the professor's attention is distracted by a question from a student or his back is turned. Be as quiet as possible.

⭐ **Sit in the back of the room.**
Avoid being jarred by loud, unpleasant noises, like your professor's voice.

⭐ **Do not rest your head.**
Do not put your head on your hand or the desk; these positions are very conducive to sleep. Sit up straight in your seat.

⭐ **Remain silent.**
Do not raise your hand or try to answer questions.

Be Aware
- To prevent a hangover, eat a combination of a banana, a sports drink, and a multivitamin after drinking/before going to class.
- An alternative way to prevent a hangover is to eat fatty foods, which coat your stomach, before drinking alcoholic beverages.
- The best way to prevent a hangover is not to drink.

HOW TO PAD
A RÉSUMÉ

⭐ Be descriptive and creative.
Employ uncommon action verbs to describe your qualifications and experience. Instead of *worked,* say *coordinated, organized,* or *interfaced.* Consult your thesaurus to avoid repetition.

⭐ Exaggerate job experiences.
Describe your previous jobs in the most sophisticated language you can. No job is unimportant. If you worked the drive-through lane at a fast-food restaurant, state that you "interacted with a diverse client base in a fast-paced environment." See the Job Description Euphemism Chart, page 158.

⭐ Quantify your experience.
If you were a peer counselor or guided new students through orientation, be specific about how many people you assisted. If you have handled money in a work or extracurricular situation, include a specific monetary amount or number of transactions. List your campus activities, no matter how trivial they may seem. Mention leadership positions within your fraternity, groups you have organized, volunteer work, or participation in protests. The more full the page looks, the better.

Job Description Euphemism Chart

What you did:	What you list:
Worked the deep fryer	Acted as sous-chef in popular lunch venue
Bagged groceries	Coordinated order fulfillment
Answered phones	Interfaced with clients
Mowed lawns	Landscaped for private clients
Made beds	Arranged accommodations for a hotel
Dug ditches	Industrial waste facilitator
Waited tables	Managed client relations
Babysat	Child development consultant
Folded clothes in department store	Sales associate in the garment industry
Gas station/ convenience store clerk	Auto mechanic's assistant
Lifeguard	Health and safety supervisor
Washed dishes	Restaurant critic
Lifted boxes in a warehouse	Inventory manager
Centerfold	Centerfold

★ **Keep your résumé to one page.**
A single page looks solid and full and makes you look more focused and experienced. Reduce the type size, change the font, or decrease the margins at the top, bottom, and sides to make it fit.

★ **Provide information strategically.**
If your grade point average is below a 3.0, do not include it. If you have a strong GPA in your concentration, list only that. List study groups you have led or special projects in which you have participated. If you include hobbies and interests, be as specific as possible.

★ **Work your contacts.**
If you or your parents know someone in the company, or if you were referred to the job by an alumnus or another contact, mention it in the first line of your cover letter.

★ **Impress with your presentation.**
Buy heavy cream linen or white laid paper and envelopes to create the impression that you are stylish and sophisticated. If you are including a writing sample, put it in a binder. Type the mailing label or envelope. Make sure the paper stock of your envelope matches that of your résumé. If you are e-mailing a résumé, be specific about the job you are applying for in the subject line. Do something to grab their attention, such as "Marketing Assistant position— YOUR SEARCH IS OVER!" Include the résumé as

an attachment to your e-mail and also cut and paste it into the body of your message to make it as easy as possible for your potential employer to read it.

Be Aware

- Check your spelling. Slowly read your résumé backward to ensure that each word is correct. Pay extra attention to your phone number and contact information.
- Make sure you have a professional-sounding outgoing phone message and that you check your e-mail account regularly. If you live in a group situation, list your cell phone number instead of your home telephone to avoid a roommate answering the phone inappropriately or failing to deliver a message.

APPENDIX

HOW TO SOUND INTELLIGENT: USEFUL NAMES

Philosophers

Aristotle	AIR-is-tot-el
Confucius	Con-FYOO-shes (like "confusion")
Descartes	Day-CART
Erasmus	Ir-ASS-muss
Kant	KAHNT
Kierkegaard	KEER-ki-guard
Machiavelli	Mock-ee-ah-VEL-lee
Nietzsche	NEE-cha
Plato	PLAY-toe
Sartre	SAR-tra
Schopenhauer	SHOW-pen-how-er
Socrates	SOCK-ra-tease
Sun Tzu	SOON ZOO

Artists

Botticelli	Bot-i-CHEL-lee
Brueghel	BROY-gull
Cézanne	Say-ZON
Chagall	Sha-GALL
Dalí	DA-lee
Da Vinci	Da VIN-chee

Degas	Day-GA
Delacroix	Del-a-QUA
Duchamp	Doo-SHAN
Gauguin	Go-GAN
Gentileschi	Gen-tile-LESS-ski
Hokusai	HOE-koo-sigh
Klee	CLAY
Magritte	Ma-GREET
Manet	Ma-NAY
Matisse	Ma-TEESE
Miró	Mee-ROW
Monet	Moan-NAY
Munch	MOONK
Raphael	RA-fay-el
Renoir	REN-war
Rodin	ROW-dan
Seurat	Se-RA
Toulouse-Lautrec	Too-LOOSE Lo-TRECK
Van Dyck	Van DIKE
Van Gogh	Van GO

NOVELISTS, POETS, AND PLAYWRIGHTS

Aristophanes	Air-is-TOF-an-ees
Baudelaire	Bode-a-LARE
Brontë	BRON-tay
Camus	Cam-OO
Capote	Ca-PO-tee
Cervantes	Sir-VON-tease
Cocteau	Cock-TOE
Dante	DON-tay

Dostoyevsky ....Dost-ta-YEF-ski
Dumas ....Doo-MA
Flaubert ....Flow-BEAR
García Márquez............Gar-SEE-ah MAR-kez
Goethe ....GER-ta
Kafka ....COUGH-ka
Kundera ....Coon-DUH-ra
Maugham.....................MOM
Molière ....Mole-YARE
Nabokov.......................Na-BOK-ov
Poe...............................PO
Pynchon ....PIN-chin
Rabelais........................RAB-a-lay
Rushdie ....RUSH-dee
Shakespeare..................SHAKE-spear
Solzhenitsyn.................Soul-jen-EAT-zen
Yeats ....YATES

HOW TO TELL YOUR PARENTS YOU'VE BEEN EXPELLED

Mom and Dad—I've got something big I need to tell you. Your baby boy/girl is coming home! And not just for a visit this time—for good.

I've decided that college just isn't working out for me. And believe me, I've discussed this with the dean, my advisors, and several professors, so I'm very sure about it. In a while I'll probably be ready to try school again, at another college, one that is a better fit for my strengths and abilities. This just wasn't the right time and place.

Due to a whole tangle of academic rules and regulations—which were part of the problem, actually—you'll be getting a letter from the dean. Officially, of course, he has to come up with some important-sounding explanations and a lot of exaggerated descriptions of what I've done and not done, and reasons for not refunding the tuition.

But that's not important. What is important is that I miss you guys, and I think that it's best if I leave school now. After all, isn't college really about figuring out who you are and want to be?

I love you both very much. Please send a plane ticket and money to the local youth hostel, where I'm now staying. I look forward to seeing you soon.
Love,
Your son/daughter

WORST-CASE SCENARIO SURVIVAL DIPLOMA

1 Place diploma on photocopier.
Lay the diploma (page 167) on the glass of the photocopier. For best results, remove the diploma from the book by cutting along the dotted line.

2 Enlarge.
Copy at 175 percent onto $8^1/_2$-x-11-inch or larger paper.

3 Write your name and the date on the photocopy.
Use a calligraphy pen to write your first, middle, and last names on the first blank line of the diploma. Write the date on the second blank line.

4 Frame.
Select an $8^1/_2$-x-11-inch frame with glass. Center the diploma (trimming the sheet of paper to fit) in the frame.

5 Hang high on a wall.
Choose a height and location that discourages close inspection.

6 Be proud.
We congratulate you.

Worst-Case University

On the nomination of the Faculty of the
School of Survival Arts, the University
has conferred upon

---

the degree of

Bachelor of Survival Arts

---

and is awarded this diploma, with all the honors and privileges pertaining herein.
In testimony whereof, the seal of the University and the signatures of those
Authorized by the University have been affixed this day.

David Borgenicht
Chairman of the Board of Trustees

Joshua Piven
President of WCU

Jennifer Worick
Dean

DON'T PANIC · BE PREPARED

THE EXPERTS

The Association of Home Appliance Manufacturers (www.aham.org).

Nicole Beland is the author of *The Cocktail Jungle* and is a former senior editor at *Cosmopolitan* and *Mademoiselle* magazines. She writes regularly for *Men's Health* and other national publications on topics ranging from sex and relationships to food and wine. She lives in Brooklyn, New York.

Shoshana Berger is editor-in-chief of *ReadyMade*, a magazine she co-founded in 2001. She has been a writer and editor for publications ranging from the *New York Times* to *Spin*.

David Blend is a freelance writer who began his career as a bar columnist for the now defunct *Met* magazine in Dallas. He has written for *Men's Journal* and *Details*, wrote the *Pocket Idiot's Guide to Tailgating*, and maintains a drinking etiquette column called "Drinking With . . ." at danm.us/blog.

Amy Calhoun, former associate director of admissions at the University of Pennsylvania, has worked with the school's University Scholars Program and in alumni giving. She currently heads the school's digital media design group.

Dominic Cappello (www.tentalks.com) designs safety, health, and communications programs for parents and educators and is the author of *Ten Talks about Violence* and the co-author of *Ten Talks about Sex and Character* and *Ten Talks About Drugs and Choices*. He is currently developing an animated television series.

"Mountain" Mel Deweese is a retired U.S. Navy Survival Evasion Resistance Escape instructor who has taught more than 100,000 students and has more than 30 years of survival training experience. He is the owner of Nature Knowledge in Grand Junction, Colorado (www.youwillsurvive.com).

Gerry Dworkin is an aquatics safety and water rescue consultant at Lifesaving Resources Inc. (www.lifesaving.com), which seeks to prevent and/or reduce the number of drownings and aquatic injuries throughout the United States through the education and training of lifeguard, aquatic safety, and recreation personnel.

Shawn Engbrecht is one of the world's top protection officers. When he is not on operational assignment, he is one of the instructors at the Center for Advanced Security Studies, specializing in the training and placement of bodyguards.

Ben Freely has been in the bar and restaurant business in Philadelphia and London for 12 years.

Rick Frishman is president of Planned Television Arts and executive vice president at Ruder*Finn. A book publicist and public speaker, he is the co-author of *Guerrilla Marketing for Writers* and *Guerrilla Publicity*.

Anthony Giglio is a New York–based wine/food/spirits writer and sommelier. He writes the "Liquids" column for *Boston Magazine* and the "Nightlife" column for *Wine & Spirits*, and is a restaurant critic for the *New York Sun*. He has also written for *Esquire*, *Details*, and *Food & Wine*.

Grace Hawthorne is publisher and CEO of *ReadyMade*, a magazine she co-founded in 2001. She has also worked as an entertainment media consultant for Trimark Pictures and Giant Robot.

Allison Hemming is the author of *Work It! How to Get Ahead, Save Your Ass and Land a Job in Any Economy*. She is an established career authority and the creator of the Pink Slip Party, a networking event that benefits the recently downsized. Hemming is also the president and "Top Gun" of The Hired Guns (www.thehiredguns.com), an interim workforce agency based in Manhattan.

Josh Herman owns Josh Herman Bail Bonds in Los Angeles (www.jhbail.com).

Dave Hill, a U.K.-based food industry consultant, advises manufacturers and caterers on safe food production. He has written numerous guides to good hygiene practice and is a fellow of the Institute of Food Science and Technology (www.ifst.org).

Chuck Hughes, author of *What It Really Takes to Get into the Ivy League* (www.roadtocollege.com), was senior admissions officer and a dorm proctor at Harvard University.

Tony Kearney is the coordinator for Undergraduate Staff Development, Office of Staff Development & Judicial Programs, Russell Hall, University of Georgia in Athens. He has lived in residence halls for 12 years as an undergraduate, a graduate student, and a professional at the University of North Carolina, the University of South Carolina, and the University of Georgia.

Ann Keith Kennedy graduated from the University of Kansas in 1990 and has been an English teacher in Japan, window display designer, architect, and librarian.

Melisa W. Lai, M.D., a former admissions officer at Brown University, is emergency medicine attending physician at Mt. Auburn Hospital in Cambridge, Massachusetts, and a fellow in clinical toxicology at the Massachusetts/Rhode Island Poison Control Center.

Bryan Lindert is a test-prep instructor for high school and college students and a social worker in south Florida. He had a perfect score on the verbal portion of his SAT.

Virginia Mattingly is a middle school teacher and the co-author of *Field Guide to Stains*.

Melissa McDaniels, M.A., has advised college students and adults for 10 years on issues related to career development, work-based conflict resolution, and job search strategies. She has worked at Boston College, Boston University, and Northeastern University, in addition to working with private clients. She is currently a doctoral student in higher, adult, and lifelong education at Michigan State University.

Tom McManus, former regional director of admissions at the University of Pennsylvania, is director of college counseling at the Tatnall School in Wilmington, Delaware.

Charlotte R. Miller is a peer mediation specialist at the Center for Professional Development & Instructional Support, part of the Harris County Department of Education in Houston, Texas. She trains teachers, counselors, and principals in the development of mediation programs.

Susan Newman, Ph.D. (www.susannewmanphd.com), is a social psychologist and the author of numerous books on social and familial relationships. She teaches at Rutgers University.

Marv Pinkey is the owner of Ten Stone, a Philadelphia bar. He has been a bartender for 15 years.

Don Rabon (www.donrabon.net), manager of the Investigations Center for the North Carolina Justice Academy, has trained investigators in interviewing and interrogation techniques in 47 states. He has also trained members of the U.S. military, the Secret Service, the CIA, and NATO forces.

Jason R. Rich (www.jasonrich.com), president of Teen Talk Communications, is the author of numerous books, including *The Everything College Survival Book*. He lives in Massachusetts.

Pete Riley was a trucker on the overnight shift for 2 years, both cross-country and on the East Coast.

Chris Robinson works at A1 Commercial & Residential Janitorial Maintenance, a cleaning services company based in Philadelphia.

Mann A. Shoffner is a former president of the Sigma chapter of Zeta Psi at the University of Pennsylvania.

The Sociology Department of the University of California at Berkeley.

Brett Stern, author of *99 Ways to Open a Beer Bottle without a Bottle Opener*, invents surgical instruments and implantable medical devices.

G. Keith Still, Ph.D., runs Crowd Dynamics Ltd. (www.crowddynamics.com), an international crowd safety and pedestrian planning and design firm based in the U.K.

Sarah Susanka, AIA, is an architect and the author of the *Not So Big House* series (www.notsobighouse.com).

Daina Taimina, Ph.D., is a math professor at Cornell University who has heard every excuse in the book.

Katherine Tallmadge, M.A., R.D., is spokesperson for the American Dietetic Association and the author of *Diet Simple: 154 Mental Tricks, Substitutions, Habits & Inspirations* (www.dietsimple.info).

Brett Thomas is a bartender at Ten Stone, a bar located in Philadelphia.

Jared Von Arx, Ph.D., is a child/adolescent clinical psychologist. He lives in Philadelphia.

ABOUT THE AUTHORS

Joshua Piven graduated from a large Ivy League university in just four-and-a-half years. He owes everything to his English professors, who choose to remain anonymous. He is the co-author, with David Borgenicht, of the *Worst-Case Scenario Survival Handbook* series.

David Borgenicht has survived dozens of collegiate nightmares, including the one where you wake up naked in the middle of an art history exam for which you haven't studied. He is the co-author, with Josh Piven, of the *Worst-Case Scenario Survival Handbook* series.

Jennifer Worick graduated from a kick-ass Big 10 school. After surviving pints of peach schnapps and countless walks of shame, she moved on to an illustrious writing career. Among her many books, she is the co-author of the *Worst-Case Scenario Survival Handbook: Dating & Sex*.

Brenda Brown is an illustrator and cartoonist whose work has been published in many books and major publications, including *The Worst-Case Scenario Survival Handbook* series, *Esquire*, *Reader's Digest*, *USA Weekend*, *21st Century Science & Technology*, *The Saturday Evening Post*, *The National Enquirer*, and many other magazines. Her website is http://webtoon.com.

Visit www.worstcasescenarios.com for updates, new scenarios, and more! Because you just never know. . . .

ACKNOWLEDGMENTS

Josh Piven thanks all of the experts, for their college knowledge; his parents, for footing the bill for his education; and the cast of the film *Animal House*, for their inspirational approach to higher learning.

David Borgenicht would like to thank his alma mater and his alma pater; his editors, Jay Schaefer, Steve Mockus, and Melissa Wagner; the entire team at Chronicle Books and Quirk Books; Frances J. Soo Ping Chow; and all the experts who contributed their, er, expertise. He'd also like to apologize for the time he started that food fight, killed the ROTC captain's horse, slept with the mayor's daughter, and ruined the big parade at the end of the movie.

Jennifer Worick would like to thank the following people: editor Melissa Wagner; co-authors Dave Borgenicht and Josh Piven, whom she sorely wishes had gone to college with her so they could have helped her research and cram for exams; all of the talented experts; and Sacha Adorno, Brenda Brown, Mindy Brown, Kerry Colburn, Josh Freely, Liesa Goins, Laurel Rivers, Alison Rooney, Jay Schaefer, Frances J. Soo Ping Chow, Ann Wilson, and all of her family and friends. She also thanks her college roommates—Maria, Donna, Janet, Amy, and Nadine— who helped her through four years with minimal damage to her liver or her sanity.

THE FIRST OF THE WORST

⚠ 3 million copies in print

⚠ Translated into 27 languages

⚠ International best-seller

"An armchair guide for the anxious."
—*USA Today*

"The book to have when the killer bees arrive."
—*The New Yorker*

"Nearly 180 pages of immediate action drills for when everything goes to hell in a handbasket."
—*Soldier of Fortune*

"This is a really nifty book."
—*Forbes*

A BOOK FOR EVERY DISASTER

- ⭐ *The Worst-Case Scenario Survival Handbook*

- ⭐ *The Worst-Case Scenario Survival Handbook:* **Travel**

- ⭐ *The Worst-Case Scenario Survival Handbook:* **Dating & Sex**

- ⭐ *The Worst-Case Scenario Survival Handbook:* **Golf**

- ⭐ *The Worst-Case Scenario Survival Handbook:* **Holidays**

- ⭐ *The Worst-Case Scenario Survival Handbook:* **Work**

- ⭐ *The Worst-Case Scenario Survival Handbook:* **Weddings**

- ⭐ *The Worst-Case Scenario Survival Handbook:* **Parenting**

- ⭐ *The Worst-Case Scenario Book of* **Survival Questions**

- ⭐ *The Worst-Case Scenario Survival Handbook:* **Extreme Edition**

- ⭐ *The Worst-Case Scenario Survival Handbook:* **Life**

- ⭐ *The Worst-Case Scenario Almanac:* **History**

- ⭐ *The Worst-Case Scenario Almanac:* **Great Outdoors**

MORE WORST-CASE SCENARIOS FOR EVERY SEASON

→ The Worst-Case Scenario Daily Survival Calendar
→ The Worst-Case Scenario Daily Survival Calendar: Golf
→ The Worst-Case Scenario Dating & Sex Address Book
→ The Worst-Case Scenario Sticky Situation Notes

Watch for these WORST-CASE SCENARIO games at retailers near you or at:

VISIT

www.chroniclebooks.com/worstcase
to order books and read excerpts

www.worstcasescenarios.com for
updates, new scenarios, and more!

Because you just never know...